Bible Immersion

A Life-Changing Way to Encounter the Word of God

Patricia D. Nordstrom

WESTBOW
PRESS®
A DIVISION OF THOMAS NELSON
& ZONDERVAN

Copyright © 2018 Patricia D. Nordstrom.

All rights reserved. No part of this book may be used or reproduced by any means, graphic, electronic, or mechanical, including photocopying, recording, taping or by any information storage retrieval system without the written permission of the author except in the case of brief quotations embodied in critical articles and reviews.

WestBow Press books may be ordered through booksellers or by contacting:

WestBow Press
A Division of Thomas Nelson & Zondervan
1663 Liberty Drive
Bloomington, IN 47403
www.westbowpress.com
1 (866) 928-1240

Because of the dynamic nature of the Internet, any web addresses or links contained in this book may have changed since publication and may no longer be valid. The views expressed in this work are solely those of the author and do not necessarily reflect the views of the publisher, and the publisher hereby disclaims any responsibility for them.

Any people depicted in stock imagery provided by Getty Images are models, and such images are being used for illustrative purposes only.
Certain stock imagery © Getty Images.

Green Wreath and Floral Border from Freepik.com.
All fonts are Times New Roman or Pink Gladiolus.

Unless otherwise cited, all scripture quotations are from the ESV® Bible (The Holy Bible, English Standard Version®), copyright © 2001 by Crossway, a publishing ministry of Good News Publishers. Used by permission. All rights reserved.

Scripture quotations marked (NIV) are taken from the Holy Bible, New International Version®, NIV®. Copyright © 1973, 1978, 1984, 2011 by Biblica, Inc.™ Used by permission of Zondervan. All rights reserved worldwide. www.zondervan.com The "NIV" and "New International Version" are trademarks registered in the United States Patent and Trademark Office by Biblica, Inc.

Scripture quotations marked (NLT) are taken from the Holy Bible, New Living Translation, copyright ©1996, 2004, 2015 by Tyndale House Foundation. Used by permission of Tyndale House Publishers, Inc., Carol Stream, Illinois 60188. All rights reserved.

ISBN: 978-1-9736-2984-9 (sc)
ISBN: 978-1-9736-2985-6 (hc)
ISBN: 978-1-9736-2983-2 (e)

Library of Congress Control Number: 2018906430

Print information available on the last page.

WestBow Press rev. date: 7/2/2018

Dedication

This book is dedicated to my Lord and Savior Jesus Christ. I thank Him for loving me. I thank Him for rescuing my soul.

I also dedicate this book to my loving husband Jeff. Our eight children (four of our own, plus their four spouses): Kurt, Amanda, Sirah, Trisha, Jacob, Christina, Alex, and Alli. And our eight grandchildren: Kat, Matthew, Sebastian, Timothy, Elliot, Nicholas, Joshua, Donovan, and Corinne.

All proceeds from this book go to The Bible for Food Recovery, Inc., a 501 (c)(3) non-profit ministry. Bible for Food is dedicated to teaching others how to acquire freedom from the stronghold of compulsive eating, through a vibrant relationship with our Lord and Savior Jesus Christ. Our members are encouraged to read, study, and apply Scripture daily. In addition they are taught to practice clear, clean, and committed abstinence. As members we choose to be disciplined in our eating so that our commitment to living out The Great Commission is never compromised.

Our website is: www.bibleforfood.org.

How this book is set up:

I. The Essentials
The scope and vision for the book
The definition of Bible Immersion
How Bible Immersion is done.

II. The Daily Pages
A place to record Bible Immersion
Making the retrieval of the insights quickly
Space for recording prayer needs of others and plans for service

III. The Readings
Further instruction on Bible Immersion
Background information about the author
The authors own insights from immersing in the word

IV. Testimonies
Bible Immersion from students' perspectives
Inspiration of students who use Bible Immersion
Encouragement to try and continue in Bible Immersion

Appendix: *Through the Bible in a Year Calendar*

CONTENTS

How this book is set up vi

Bible Immersion Essentials 1

1. The Purpose of This Book 2
2. Called to Be Light Bringers 3
3. Twenty-four Hours of Potential 5
4. What is Bible Immersion? 7
5. Let's Get Started 9
6. Scripture, Thoughts, and Prayer 15

Quick Start to Bible Immersion 19

Daily Pages for Your Bible Immersion 20

Readings to Help You Stay on Course 221

1. Reading Through the Bible Each Year 222
2. Pray Without Ceasing 224
3. My Weapon Against Overeating and Depression 227
4. God's Daily Reminders 229
5. Fear Not 231
6. Remembering the Call Upon My Life 233
7. Don't Fool Yourself! 234
8. My Great High Priest 235
9. Showing True Love and Compassion 236
10. Seeking God First 237
11. There's Nothing My God Cannot Do! 238

12. When Sheep Rebel 239
13. Read. Study. Apply. 240
14. Unbelief 242
15. Deeper Waters 243
16. My Bible Immersion Story 244
17. Standing Firm Through Hard Times....................................246
18. The Way, the Truth, the Life 248
19. Workers of Evil..249
20. Build Each Other Up 251
21. Keeping the Main Thing the Main Thing 252
22. Diversion 253
23. Marching Orders 254
24. My Help Comes from the Lord 255
25. Rising Above the Flesh 256
26. Standing Firm 257
27. True Inspiration 258
28. Speak Life...259
29. Ungodly Counsel 260
30. The Best Way 261
31. Most Important..262
32. God's Wonderful Truth 264
33. Favoritism 265
34. Keeping the Lord the Highest Priority 266
35. Walk Away from the Tube...267
36. Relapse—Bible Style..269
37. Light to All 270
38. Good Work. God's Work. 271
39. Solomon's Downfall 272
40. When Faced with Physical Pain 274

41. Aborting a Return to Sinful Behavior 276
42. Ugly and Despicable 278
43. Living Water 280
44. Sadly Mistaken 282
45. How to Use the Bible as an Inventory Tool 284
46. Keeping the Right Size 286
47. How to Have an Abstinent Day 287
48. The Living, Active, Powerful Word of God 289
49. When the Goings Get Tough 291
50. Verses and Prayers to Fight Discouragement 293

Testimonies and Examples of Scripture, Thoughts, and Prayer 295

Ellen, New York 296
Eunice, Ohio 296
Carrie, Washington 297
Tammy, Georgia 298
Dawn, Massachusetts 299
Annette, Texas 300
Kim, Georgia 301
Danielle, New York 302
Dorothea, New York 303
Deanna, Florida 304
Dorothea, California 305
Sherri, New Jersey 306
Bridget, Hawaii 307
April, New York 308
Drena, Maryland 310
Debbie, Indiana 311
Kathleen, California 312
Sharon, Virginia 312

Mindy, California 313
Patricia, Maryland 315
Meechie, Maryland 316
Jasmine, Washington D.C. 317
Laura, New York 318
Jill, Connecticut 319
Wanda, Maryland 320
Lydia, Virginia 321
Robin, Ohio 321
Mary, New York 322
Myesha, Maryland 323
Barbara, New Jersey 324
Diann, New Jersey 325
Rebecca, California 325
Daily Page Example 328
Through the Bible in a Year   **332**

1

THE PURPOSE OF THIS BOOK

If you know these things, blessed are you if you do them.
~ John 13:17

The purpose of this book is to share with you a very simple yet effective way to study the Bible that I call Bible Immersion. I have practiced this method for over 26 years. I have taught it to individuals, in classes, through workshops, and in seminars. It is easy to learn, and I have seen it bring about life-changing results in both me and in my students.

The best way to learn Bible Immersion is to jump in and try it. Therefore, this book will invite you to become interactive in learning it. After you have gotten the gist of the "how to" of the technique, I encourage you to begin using Bible Immersion each day. Nothing that I write will convince you of how life-changing it is like your own firsthand experience. Most who use it consistently for just three weeks, are amazed! My prayer is that God will capture your heart as you sense His closeness and deep love for you through immersing in His word.

CALLED TO BE LIGHT BRINGERS

For at one time you were darkness, but now you are light in the Lord. Walk as children of light. ~ Ephesians 5:8

In a dark world, we have been called to live lives that draw others to Jesus. We are compared to a city on a hill that cannot be hidden (*Matthew 5:14*). We should shine in ways that cause the unsaved to step back and take note of our lives. In the book of Acts is an example of what I mean. It shows how uneducated fishermen become transformed to be bold men of God (*Acts 2-4*).

The narrative unfolds: Jesus has returned to His Father, but not without leaving the promised gift of the indwelling Holy Spirit. In the power of the Holy Spirit, Peter heals a man who has been lame since birth. Not surprisingly, the word spreads like wildfire and the crowd comes to see with their own eyes what has happened. Peter uses this opportunity to preach the Good News of Jesus Christ.

Peter speaks with boldness about Our Lord and Savior, Jesus. His sermon causes the number of new believers to reach an all-time high of 5,000 men. When the rulers behold the confidence of Peter, and of John who is with him, they are blown away: *Now when they saw the boldness of Peter and John, and perceived that they were uneducated, common men, they were astonished. And they recognized that they had been with Jesus. ~ Acts 4:13*

And this is the point. If we are going to be light-bringers into the world, we must spend significant heart-to-heart time with Jesus. Jesus is revealed through learning Scripture and living it out. Therefore Bible study cannot be a hit-or-miss endeavor. It must be daily and purposeful.

TWENTY-FOUR HOURS OF POTENTIAL

Many, Lord my God, are the wonders you have done, the things you planned for us. None can compare with you; were I to speak and tell of your deeds, they would be too many to declare. ~ Psalm 40:5

As human beings we start each day with 24 hours. Those of us who are adults have control over how our hours will be spent. If I say that I love Jesus and I want to be like Him, then it follows that I need to make the time to learn about Him and to hear from Him. The Bible is the unmistakable place where this learning can occur.

Each day I need an intuitive, hands-on way to get into the word of God. I need to be drawn in so that I keep coming back to Scripture. I need to engage not only my mind, but my heart and emotions as well. I need to hear God speak directly to me and into my affairs.

This happens in Bible Immersion and more. It is practical and captivating. It has made the study of Scripture a delightful "want to" as opposed to a dreary "have to". I have heard more than a few students ask that I pray for them to stay with Bible Immersion for the rest of their lives. And I do pray for them, because my prayer is the same for me! I never want to turn my back on this God-given treasure because the growth that Bible Immersion has brought about in my life is incredible!

{Dear Father, please fill me up with your Holy Spirit so that I might show others what You have shown to me. Your word is truly powerful and active. Living out Your word gives me a life beyond my wildest dreams. Living out Your word brings healing into my world. Thank you for the Bible. Thank you for the Holy Spirit who opens up its meaning to my heart. In the name of Jesus I pray. Amen.}

WHAT IS BIBLE IMMERSION?

This Book of the Law shall not depart from your mouth, but you shall meditate on it day and night, so that you may be careful to do according to all that is written in it. For then you will make your way prosperous, and then you will have good success. ~ Joshua 1:8

Bible Immersion is the systematic practice of reading through the whole Bible each year, combined with deeply studying the Bible each day. This daily study includes finding a heart connection with a section of Scripture, writing about this connection, and praying sincerely for change.

Bible Immersion takes seriously that *"all scripture is God-breathed" (2 Timothy 3:16-17)*. It stands upon the belief that God is speaking to His children through His word. It stands upon the fact that every born-again believer has the indwelling Holy Spirit. Therefore, every sincere encounter with a significant amount of Scripture will reveal a message for the believer. Serious students of Bible Immersion come to the word each time expecting to meet Jesus, and they are not disappointed!

Bible Immersion draws the student into the whole word of God. When practiced consistently, the student begins seeing changes in their emotional responses to life's circumstances. They become more peaceful. They are able to make wiser and more decisive choices. They see their faith growing.

Each day I can count on Bible Immersion to reset my thinking back to Truth. I am kept standing strong in my faith—maintaining a passionate gratitude for my salvation. Each time that I am done with Bible Immersion I feel better. And if I do not feel better, then I know that I am not done! God speaks to me through His word and I am learning to reprioritize my life so that I do not go out into my day without this vital time with my Savior.

{Dear Father, grow me up to become strong in You. May I see the beauty in your commands; they lead me to the best life possible! Keep me growing in the love of Your word as I see the changes that are occurring in my life. I pray to speak, think, and live out Your word, in the power of the Spirit, more and more each day. In the name of Jesus Christ I pray. Amen.}

YOUR ASSIGNMENT	
	• Find a Bible that you are willing to write in and mark up. Get a translation that speaks to your heart. If you are absolutely new at choosing a Bible, this article on the Lifeway website might be helpful to you: http://www.lifeway.com/Article/How-to-choose-the-right-bible
	• Begin praying for yourself and asking others to pray for your willingness to give the Bible Immersion technique a genuine attempt. Pray that you will try it the first part of your day. Pray that you will do each assignment with sincerity. Pray that you will try each assignment in the book before deciding that Bible Immersion is not for you.

LET'S GET STARTED

But the Helper, the Holy Spirit, whom the Father will send in my name, he will teach you all things and bring to your remembrance all that I have said to you. ~ John 14:26

1. PRAY FOR A FILLING OF THE HOLY SPIRIT

The first step for any effective time in the word is fervent prayer. I ask, therefore, that you stop reading, bow your head, and engage your heart. Ask the Father to give you an earnest filling of the Holy Spirit. Let Him know that you desire to hear and understand the lesson that He has for you in His word. Ask that when you finish your Bible Immersion time, you will have the willingness and the strength to walk out in faith, in this very day, to do the things that He reveals.

2. DECIDE WHAT SCRIPTURE YOU WILL READ

You will need a day by day assignment. Keep in mind, one of the key components to Bible Immersion is the willingness to make reading through the Bible each year a life-long discipline. In order to do this, you will need to read about three chapters of the Bible each day. If you search the web, you can find many "Through the Bible in a Year" reading schedules. I prefer one that assigns daily readings in both the Old and the New Testaments. If you are in need of a plan, there is one found at the end of this book. You can also find this plan on the BibleForFood.org homepage. Click on the "daily reading" tab and you will see it.

I have learned that reading a substantial amount of Scripture each day is imperative in circumventing the attack that is waged on my mind for being a Christ follower. I don't believe that I am unique as a Christian to have this attack. When anyone becomes serious about Jesus, this attack is to be expected. Scripture is the "sword of the Spirit" (see ***Ephesians 6:17b***). I must purposefully arm myself with God's word in order to navigate successfully through this day to day life.

We live in a culture where people are slaves to their emotions. We have become a people where our feelings dictate what we do. Scripture can stop the attack. I have heard it preached that our emotions should be the caboose, and not the engine of our lives. We have become a society of people where we base our volition on our emotions. As a Christian, this is so very wrong! The Lord is my guiding force. He must empower and dictate what I do and what I don't do. Scripture reminds me of what is important to do and how, with God, I can get things done. As a Born Again believer, I have the Holy Spirit living in me. I have access to the same power that brought Jesus back to life! This is the power that should be running my life and not emotions that have been birthed by erroneous thinking.

When I read Scripture I feed spiritual transformation (see ***Romans 12:2***). Even when I do not totally understand what I am reading and hearing in the word, Scripture is still changing me and growing me:

> *As the rain and the snow come down from heaven, and do not return to it without watering the earth and making it bud and flourish, so that it yields seed for the sower and bread for the eater, so is my word that goes out from my mouth: It will not return to me empty, but will accomplish what I desire and achieve the purpose for which I sent it.*
> *~ Isaiah 55:10-11*

My emotions are controlled by my thinking. If I allow the lies of Satan to linger in my thoughts, I will eventually feel negativity, rage, bitterness, and the like. When I allow the truth of God to linger in my thoughts I feel the strength, power, and motivation of the Lord. Through the years I have learned the importance that I read Scripture, hear Scripture, think Scripture, write about Scripture, pray Scripture, and memorize the word of God.

3. FIND AN AUDIO VERSION OF YOUR SCRIPTURE ASSIGNMENT

The Bible states that *faith comes by hearing (Romans 10:17)*. I find that when I listen to Scripture as I read, I get help to keep moving along. Listening as I read also helps me to learn the correct pronunciation of the names and places in Scripture.

Before, when I would just read the assignment, I would sometimes never get around to completing it. I would find myself spending time searching commentaries and not trusting that God was going to explain things in time. (I was not unlike the elementary student waving his hand to ask the question that the teacher was preparing to address just before she was interrupted!) I will state it again: listening as I read keeps me moving along. I have to trust that getting an overview will help me to have a clearer picture of what I am reading. The Bible is one marvelous story of God's love for mankind!

Many Christians have completed many Bible studies, but have never read certain books in the Bible. These less popular chapters and books are just a sacred as the others. *2 Timothy 3:16* reminds us that *all Scripture is God-breathed*! When it comes to His word, God desires that I learn from ALL that He has provided.

4. WHILE READING AND LISTENING, UNDERLINE

As God is speaking to me, I underline all the places that catch my eye. Later I look over these highlighted words, phrases, or verses to find my selected "growing place" for the day.

God speaks to me through the words of Scripture. When doing my Bible Immersion I sometimes picture myself being in a large lecture hall. The speaker (the Lord) has a message for my day which is going to take away the thoughts and feelings that would tell me to run away and hide from life. These thoughts are vicious and at one time in my life, this same type of thinking led to addictive behaviors, hurtful habits and hidden sin.

When I first started doing Bible Immersion I would have very few things underlined as I read. I look back now and understand what was going on. The Bible was teaching me a new language. It was teaching me the language of the redeemed. Up until that time I "spoke" fluent flesh! The Bible was unfamiliar, and like many new beginnings, doing Bible Immersion took a determined effort. It was far from what it is for me today. Then it was a new discipline and being new, it was not pleasant but painful (***see Hebrews 12:10-12***). By God's grace, I did not give up!

I will share with you a very important secret to making it through a Bible-in-a-year schedule. It is this: DO NOT TRY TO CATCH UP! Realize that Bible Immersion is a lifelong discipline. What is missed this year will be covered again on future rounds. Each day I have learned that God has a message that will speak into my present life's situations and circumstances. I expect to get nourished daily and I am not disappointed.

I have come to treasure the word of God ***more than my portion of food (Job 23:12)***! Even when I was battling stage IV esophageal cancer, I knew the importance of getting my mind in the right place each day. Some thought I was crazy as I would weakly make myself over to the desk to "think, write, and pray" over the word of God. But even if they did not understand, I knew that I would be a "sitting duck" for Satan if I did not prepare my mind for the daily bodily pain that I had to deal with in that season of my life. For two years and counting at this writing, God has given me an unexpected healing on this side of heaven! Through Bible Immersion I became certain that God would heal me. I also knew that it might not be before He took me to be with Him. But His word assured me (and still assures me) that because of the blood of Jesus that covers me, my life is forever a "win-win" proposition!

5. SELECT AN ITEM OF SCRIPTURE, EXPLORE YOUR THOUGHTS, AND WRITE

When I have completed reading and listening to my full assignment, I survey the things I have underlined and I choose one. I then begin thinking deeply about what the words are saying, and how they are resonating in me. I then write from my heart.

When teaching Bible Immersion, I usually instruct people to answer one or both of these questions: 1) What does this underlined word, verse or passage bring to mind? and/or 2) What might God be saying to me?

If a student has trouble writing, I sometimes have them write on an amplification of these queries: What are some of the things that come to your mind as you think deeply about this verse or passage? What insights do you learn about God and your relationship to Him? What insights do you learn about yourself and how you are changing and growing in Christ? What convictions have surfaced? What might God be saying to You?

Another way that I have helped my students is through a method that I learned in preparation for being a volunteer at a Franklin Graham crusade. This method is a paraphrase method and has three steps: 1) Circle what you believe to be the key words of your chosen verse. 2) Use an online dictionary to look up the definition of the words and write down these definitions. 3) Use what has been learned through defining the key words and write a paraphrase of the Scripture.

In this technique, the words circled in step 1 are the student's choice. In step 2, the type of dictionary used can make quite a difference in unlocking insights. I suggest an older dictionary such as the online 1828 Webster's dictionary.

6. WRITE A PRAYER AND THEN SINCERELY PRAY AUDIBLY TO THE LORD—MAKING HEARTFELT REQUESTS AND THANKSGIVINGS

Sometimes I have been extremely surprised where my Bible Immersion time takes me. Many times it unearths hidden emotions and behaviors that would not have come to light if I had not taken the time to be interacting with Scripture in this manner. Bible Immersion allows God to work in my life. I am able to take off my teacher hat, my mother hat, my wife hat etc. It's about my time with God and allowing His word to be a moving force in my life.

{Dear Father, I can hear in my mind the words of the old hymn "I Come to the Garden Alone". And the song is true. You walk with me. You talk with me. You tell me that I am your own. And I realize that this is what happens whenever I immerse in Your word. You want to speak to my unobstructed heart. I willingly bring it to You. Please change me now. I want to be like Your Son Jesus. Make me holy for You. It is in the name of Jesus that I pray. Amen.}

6

SCRIPTURE, THOUGHTS, AND PRAYER

The truth that God reveals through His word is meant to be shared for the growth and edification of others. An effective way that I have found to share my "nuggets" is by what I call "Scripture, Thoughts, and Prayer".

I begin by writing out the verse (or a part of the verse) that will be my place of connection. I follow this with bullet points of thoughts that come to me as I aim to recall what God has taught me. I like recording what comes to me in bullet points because then I am freed from grammatical restrictions of connectedness.

Many times my thoughts seem random, but as I write them down and read them all over, they are often not as random as they first appear! Many times my "STPs" are short—one or two thoughts followed by a prayer. Sometimes they can be quite long. Sometimes I am reminded of another verse and I include this verse or the "address" of the verse into my bulleted thoughts.

When I am done thinking, I focus on my feelings. I want to record how I can cry out to the Lord about all that has been stirred up in my heart from my writing. I write this prayer, and then I pray it audibly to myself.

Examples are as follows:

1 Kings 3:6 *~ And Solomon said, "You have shown great and steadfast love to your servant David my father, because he walked before you in faithfulness, in righteousness, and in uprightness of heart toward you. And you have kept for him this great and steadfast love and have given him a son to sit on his throne this day.*

- There was much in David's life that under the scrutiny of an enemy's eye, would be seen to outweigh any good.
- But Solomon, David's son who loved him, did not see his father that way. He remembered his father as walking "in faithfulness, in righteousness, and in uprightness of heart" toward God.
- Thank God for the children who see our hearts!
- *{Dear Father, I pray that my life will be a witness of faithfulness for my children and their children when I am no longer here. May I leave a legacy that points people to You. Keep me focused on Jesus. Keep me serving Him all the days of my life! In the name of Jesus Christ I pray. Amen.}*

Psalm 37:1-3 *~ Fret not yourself because of evildoers; be not envious of wrongdoers! For they will soon fade like the grass and wither like the green herb. Trust in the* L<small>ORD</small>*, and do good; dwell in the land and befriend faithfulness.*

- The way of the world is to trust our senses. The way of God is to walk by faith. (***2 Corinthians 5:7***)
- I have to remind myself, "Don't let what you see fool you!"
- God's word states clearly—what is seen is temporary; what is unseen is eternal! (***2 Corinthians 4:18***)
- *{Dear Father, life often seems out of control. Those who cheat, lie, and steal seem to be winning and running away with the spoil! Regardless of what meets my eye, Your Spirit in me assures me of Your control. You are my eternal sovereign. I stand on the truth of Your word and Your peace encompasses me. I give You thanks in the name of Jesus. Amen.}*

Proverbs 3:5-6 ~ Trust in the LORD ***with all your heart, and do not lean on your own understanding. In all your ways acknowledge him, and he will make straight your paths.***

- God surpasses what my mind can comprehend and grasp.
- A wise Bible teacher once said: "Don't let what you don't know, stand in the way of what you do know!"
- What I do know is that God loves me and He is guiding me.
- What I do know is that this love is deep and eternal and can never be taken away from me. (**Romans 8:38-39**)
- *{Dear Father, who am I, that You chose me to experience such a wondrous love as this! I trust You because I know Your love for me to be unshakable. Keep me sitting at Your feet and drinking in Your truth—each and every day. Thank you for providing pathways of peace in a chaotic world. In the name of Jesus I pray. Amen.}*

Isaiah 40:11 ~ He tends his flock like a shepherd: He gathers the lambs in His arms and carries them close to His heart; He gently leads those that have young.

- My powerful Lord is at the same time tender and gentle. I am His lamb and He carries me close to His heart. He is my steadfast deliverer and protector. I have nothing to fear.
- *{Dear Father, thank you for caring for me in such a deep and loving, and powerful way. I trust that Your hand is all over my affairs. I trust Your protection, because You have shown me Your heart. In the name of Jesus I give praise and I pray. Amen.}*

Ezekiel 12:7 ~ I brought out my baggage at dusk, carrying it on my shoulder in their sight.

- Ezekiel was commanded to show the rebellious Israelites what it was going to be like when they were exiled. Ezekiel obeyed God and performed the pantomime. He was labeled a doomsayer by the people.

- God often gives commands to the believer that run counter to logic and/or popular opinion.
- Many people still do not understand why keeping faithful to disciplined eating is so important in my life.
- It can really be a challenge when people see me, now in a normal body size, and still practicing diligence with my choices of foods and amounts.
- *{Thank you, Father, for the conviction that You have given to me regarding abstinence. You have shown me the true nature of my former relationship with food. How I lusted after food. How I obsessed about eating. How I squandered both money and time pursing the belly god **(Philippians 3:19)**. I pray to remember that my highest goal today is to please You. Keep me faithfully growing in my knowledge and love of Jesus. It's in His name that I pray. Amen.}*

Matthew 15:1-2 ~ The Pharisees and scribes came to Jesus from Jerusalem...

- People from many places were hearing of Jesus and His ministry. Some believed Him to be the Messiah and the healing prophet. But not the Jewish leaders. At this point they had rejected Jesus and they came to Him only for the purpose of discrediting His ministry.
- We are Christians—people who have been called to follow in the footsteps of Jesus. It is a given then, that we will experience persecution, rejection, criticism, and the like.
- *{Dear Father, grow us up so that we can stand firm when others come out against the message that You have given us to bring. Let us be committed to blameless living. Let us resolve not to become bitter and begin fighting the wrong enemy. We pray to keep our eyes on Jesus, in the power of the Spirit. We pray in Jesus' name. Amen.}*

Quick Start to Bible Immersion

- Ask to be filled with the Holy Spirit so that you hear and understand what God is saying in His word.
- **While listening and reading, underline anything that stands out or speaks to your heart.
- Journal:
  - a) What does it bring to mind? and/or
  - b) What might God be saying to me?
  - **If you are having trouble thinking and writing, consider these queries: What insights do you learn about God and your relationship to Him? What insights do you learn about yourself and how you are changing and growing in Christ? What convictions have surfaced? What might God be saying to You?**
- Write a prayer, and then pray it aloud to the Lord.
- If time allows, record your insights and revelations in a "Scripture, Thoughts, Prayer" format.

Daily Pages for Your Bible Immersion

At this point it is important that you begin practicing immersing in the word. Using the reading schedule found at the back of this book and the daily pages that follow, begin your own testimony of how life-changing Bible Immersion can be. The two sections that follow this one have readings and testimonies to help deepen your commitment to Bible Immersion. But keep in mind, the best way to become convinced is to "make Bible Immersion a priority, do it sincerely, and do it consistently". You will not regret it!

These things happened to them as an example, but they were written down for our instruction, on whom the end of the ages has come. ~ 1 Corinthians 10:11

1. TODAY'S DATE August 15, 2022

- [ ] Write down 1-3 issues that are presently dominating your thoughts and hindering your concentration.

  Starting my new job

- [ ] Ask the Lord to move you away from these concerns, and to center your thoughts on Him. Ask to be filled with the Holy Spirit so that you hear and understand what God is saying in His word.

- [ ] On the line below, write your assignment for today (Or choose 3 new Bible chapters to read.)

  Psalm 90-95   1 Cor. 3

- [ ] Find an audio version of your reading assignment.

- [ ] While listening and reading, underline anything that catches your attention.

- [ ] Choose a verse, write down the address, and a few primary words from which will be your area of concentration.

- [ ] Journal on: (a) What comes to mind when reading over your Scripture selection, and/or (b) What might God be saying to you regarding your life and your issues in the light of these Scriptures?

- [ ] Write a prayer, and then pray it aloud to the Lord.

- [ ] If time allows, share your insights in a "Scripture, Thoughts, Prayer" format with others.

🌿 NOTES, PLANS, AND PRAYERS FOR OTHERS 🌿

*{Dear Father, one day Jesus will come back to take me to be where He is (**John 14: 3**). As I wait His return, I pray to live a life that pleases You. Please keep me immersed in Your word each day. Please keep me trained and equipped—teaching others to do the same. In the name of Jesus I pray. Amen.}*

Be anxious for nothing, but in everything by prayer and supplication with thanksgiving let your requests be made known to God. And the peace of God, which surpasses all comprehension, will guard your hearts and your minds in Christ Jesus. ~ Philippians 4:6

2. TODAY'S DATE_____

- ☐ Write down 1-3 issues that are presently dominating your thoughts and hindering your concentration. _new job, eating matza bread_ _____
  _____
  _____
  _____
  _____

- ☐ Ask the Lord to move you away from these concerns, and to center your thoughts on Him. Ask to be filled with the Holy Spirit so that you hear and understand what God is saying in His word.

- ☐ On the line below, write your assignment for today (Or choose 3 new Bible chapters to read) _Pslm 102-104 & 1Cor 5_

- ☐ Find an audio version of your reading assignment.

- ☐ While listening and reading, underline anything that catches your attention.

- ☐ Choose a verse, write down the address, and a few primary words from which will be your area of concentration.

- ☐ Journal on: (a) What comes to mind when reading over your Scripture selection, and/or (b) What might God be saying to you regarding your life and your issues in the light of these Scriptures?

- ☐ Write a prayer, and then pray it aloud to the Lord.

- ☐ If time allows, share your insights in a "Scripture, Thoughts, Prayer" format with others.

PS 102
That the Lord not leave me

❦ NOTES, PLANS, AND PRAYERS FOR OTHERS ❦

{Dear Father, I have been sitting here struggling, and I forgot that I don't need to struggle but to pray with fervency and belief. Empower me to do both of these things. You can do this! Give me the willingness and strength to pray until the temptation passes. In the name of Jesus I pray. Amen.}

For the word of God is living and active, sharper than any two-edged sword, piercing to the division of soul and of spirit, of joints and of marrow, and discerning the thoughts and intentions of the heart.~ Hebrews 4:12

3. TODAY'S DATE _____

- ☐ Write down 1-3 issues that are presently dominating your thoughts and hindering your concentration. _____
  _____
  _____
  _____
  _____
  _____
  _____

- ☐ Ask the Lord to move you away from these concerns, and to center your thoughts on Him. Ask to be filled with the Holy Spirit so that you hear and understand what God is saying in His word.

- ☐ On the line below, write your assignment for today (Or choose 3 new Bible chapters to read.)
  _____

- ☐ Find an audio version of your reading assignment.

- ☐ While listening and reading, underline anything that catches your attention.

- ☐ Choose a verse, write down the address, and a few primary words from which will be your area of concentration.

- ☐ Journal on: (a) What comes to mind when reading over your Scripture selection, and/or (b) What might God be saying to you regarding your life and your issues in the light of these Scriptures?

- ☐ Write a prayer, and then pray it aloud to the Lord.

- ☐ If time allows, share your insights in a "Scripture, Thoughts, Prayer" format with others.

❧ NOTES, PLANS, AND PRAYERS FOR OTHERS ❧

*{Dear Father, You are showing me how to live. Your word is truly becoming a lamp to my feet and a light for my path (**Psalm 119:105**). Thank you for showing me how to soundly defeat overeating and depression. There is NOTHING Your word cannot do! I pray to keep immersing in Your word. I pray to keep encouraging others to do the same. In the name of Jesus I pray. Amen.}*

The people of Judah have sinned again and again, and I will not let them go unpunished. They have rejected the instruction of the Lord, refusing to obey his decrees. They have been led astray by the same lies that deceived their ancestors. ~ Amos 2:4

4. TODAY'S DATE _____

- ☐ Write down 1-3 issues that are presently dominating your thoughts and hindering your concentration. _my baby goats and eating correctly_ _____
  _____
  _____
  _____
  _____

- ☐ Ask the Lord to move you away from these concerns, and to center your thoughts on Him. Ask to be filled with the Holy Spirit so that you hear and understand what God is saying in His word.

- ☐ On the line below, write your assignment for today (Or choose 3 new Bible chapters to read.)
  _____

- ☐ Find an audio version of your reading assignment.

- ☐ While listening and reading, underline anything that catches your attention.

- ☐ Choose a verse, write down the address, and a few primary words from which will be your area of concentration.

- ☐ Journal on: (a) What comes to mind when reading over your Scripture selection, and/or (b) What might God be saying to you regarding your life and your issues in the light of these Scriptures?

- ☐ Write a prayer, and then pray it aloud to the Lord.

- ☐ If time allows, share your insights in a "Scripture, Thoughts, Prayer" format with others.

🌿 NOTES, PLANS, AND PRAYERS FOR OTHERS 🌿

{Dear Father, You have left us here to tell others that the curse has been broken! Help us to remember that our primary purpose is The Great Commission. The world must see Your resurrection power demonstrated in our own lives. They must know that it is possible for them to have this power as well. Raise us up to resist the many temptations which threaten to lead us astray in this very day. Keep us out of denial and believing that we are too busy to stay immersed in your word! In the name of Jesus we pray. Amen.}

I have called you by name, you are mine. When you pass through the waters, I will be with you; and through the rivers, they shall not overwhelm you; when you walk through fire you shall not be burned, and the flame shall not consume you. For I am the LORD your God. ~ Isaiah 43:1-3

5. TODAY'S DATE_____

- ☐ Write down 1-3 issues that are presently dominating your thoughts and hindering your concentration. _____
  _____
  _____
  _____
  _____
  _____

- ☐ Ask the Lord to move you away from these concerns, and to center your thoughts on Him. Ask to be filled with the Holy Spirit so that you hear and understand what God is saying in His word.

- ☐ On the line below, write your assignment for today (Or choose 3 new Bible chapters to read.)
  _____

- ☐ Find an audio version of your reading assignment.

- ☐ While listening and reading, underline anything that catches your attention.

- ☐ Choose a verse, write down the address, and a few primary words from which will be your area of concentration.

- ☐ Journal on: (a) What comes to mind when reading over your Scripture selection, and/or (b) What might God be saying to you regarding your life and your issues in the light of these Scriptures?

- ☐ Write a prayer, and then pray it aloud to the Lord.

- ☐ If time allows, share your insights in a "Scripture, Thoughts, Prayer" format with others.

🌿 NOTES, PLANS, AND PRAYERS FOR OTHERS 🌿

{Dear Father, I pray to give You quality time in this day so that You can do Your healing work in me. I pray to read Your word. I pray to study Your word. I pray to use Your word to direct every aspect of my life. Speak to my heart. Renew my mind. Fan up the gratitude for my salvation and the passion to make You known. With all my heart, I pray to never forget this magnificent privilege of being Your child. My name is written in heaven. I have crossed over from death to life. I am eternally grateful! In the name of Jesus I give thanks and praise. Amen.}

And he said to them, "Go into all the world and proclaim the gospel to the whole creation. ~ Mark 16:15

6. TODAY'S DATE_____

- ☐ Write down 1-3 issues that are presently dominating your thoughts and hindering your concentration. _____
_____
_____
_____
_____
_____
_____

- ☐ Ask the Lord to move you away from these concerns, and to center your thoughts on Him. Ask to be filled with the Holy Spirit so that you hear and understand what God is saying in His word.

- ☐ On the line below, write your assignment for today (Or choose 3 new Bible chapters to read.)
_____

- ☐ Find an audio version of your reading assignment.

- ☐ While listening and reading, underline anything that catches your attention.

- ☐ Choose a verse, write down the address, and a few primary words from which will be your area of concentration.

- ☐ Journal on: (a) What comes to mind when reading over your Scripture selection, and/or (b) What might God be saying to you regarding your life and your issues in the light of these Scriptures?

- ☐ Write a prayer, and then pray it aloud to the Lord.

- ☐ If time allows, share your insights in a "Scripture, Thoughts, Prayer" format with others.

❧ NOTES, PLANS, AND PRAYERS FOR OTHERS ❧

{Dear Father, open my eyes to the magnificence of my salvation! Though I was one who came to You late in life, You have not withheld any of the bounty that You lavish upon Your children. Thank you for Your favor. Thank you for giving me a new life that is eternally full and meaningful. In the name of Jesus I give thanks and pray. Amen.}

The pride of your heart has deceived you, you who live in the clefts of the rock, in your lofty dwelling, who say in your heart, "Who will bring me down to the ground?" Though you soar aloft like the eagle, though your nest is set among the stars, from there I will bring you down, declares the Lord.
~ Obadiah 1:3-4

7. TODAY'S DATE_____

☐ Write down 1-3 issues that are presently dominating your thoughts and hindering your concentration. _____
_____
_____
_____
_____

☐ Ask the Lord to move you away from these concerns, and to center your thoughts on Him. Ask to be filled with the Holy Spirit so that you hear and understand what God is saying in His word.

☐ On the line below, write your assignment for today (Or choose 3 new Bible chapters to read.)
_____

☐ Find an audio version of your reading assignment.

☐ While listening and reading, underline anything that catches your attention.

☐ Choose a verse, write down the address, and a few primary words from which will be your area of concentration.

☐ Journal on: (a) What comes to mind when reading over your Scripture selection, and/or (b) What might God be saying to you regarding your life and your issues in the light of these Scriptures?

☐ Write a prayer, and then pray it aloud to the Lord.

☐ If time allows, share your insights in a "Scripture, Thoughts, Prayer" format with others.

❦ NOTES, PLANS, AND PRAYERS FOR OTHERS ❦

{Dear Father, help me to remember that love is a much better teacher than pain! Fill me up with the Holy Spirit so that I might have the willingness and strength to keep in step with the Spirit. In the name of Jesus I pray. Amen.}

The priest shall make atonement for him before the LORD, and he shall be forgiven for any of the things that one may do and thereby become guilty. ~ Leviticus 6:7

8. TODAY'S DATE_____

☐ Write down 1-3 issues that are presently dominating your thoughts and hindering your concentration. ~~Josh~~ & my ~~&~~ preparing lunches + dinners

☐ Ask the Lord to move you away from these concerns, and to center your thoughts on Him. Ask to be filled with the Holy Spirit so that you hear and understand what God is saying in His word.

☐ On the line below, write your assignment for today (Or choose 3 new Bible chapters to read.)

☐ Find an audio version of your reading assignment.

☐ While listening and reading, underline anything that catches your attention.

☐ Choose a verse, write down the address, and a few primary words from which will be your area of concentration.

☐ Journal on: (a) What comes to mind when reading over your Scripture selection, and/or (b) What might God be saying to you regarding your life and your issues in the light of these Scriptures?

☐ Write a prayer, and then pray it aloud to the Lord.

☐ If time allows, share your insights in a "Scripture, Thoughts, Prayer" format with others.

🌿 NOTES, PLANS, AND PRAYERS FOR OTHERS 🌿

{Dear Lord, Your grace is amazing to me. It speaks to me of Your great, great love for me. This love compels me to turn from my sin and live a life again that is pleasing to You. This love causes me to want to share with others, this same love that You pour into me. Thank you for being my great High Priest. May I sing of Your love forever!}

Therefore be imitators of God, as beloved children. And walk in love, as Christ loved us and gave himself up for us, a fragrant offering and sacrifice to God. ~ Ephesians 5:1-2

9. TODAY'S DATE _____

- ☐ Write down 1-3 issues that are presently dominating your thoughts and hindering your concentration. _____
  _____
  _____
  _____
  _____
  _____
  _____

- ☐ Ask the Lord to move you away from these concerns, and to center your thoughts on Him. Ask to be filled with the Holy Spirit so that you hear and understand what God is saying in His word.

- ☐ On the line below, write your assignment for today (Or choose 3 new Bible chapters to read.)
  _____

- ☐ Find an audio version of your reading assignment.

- ☐ While listening and reading, underline anything that catches your attention.

- ☐ Choose a verse, write down the address, and a few primary words from which will be your area of concentration.

- ☐ Journal on: (a) What comes to mind when reading over your Scripture selection, and/or (b) What might God be saying to you regarding your life and your issues in the light of these Scriptures?

- ☐ Write a prayer, and then pray it aloud to the Lord.

- ☐ If time allows, share your insights in a "Scripture, Thoughts, Prayer" format with others.

❧ NOTES, PLANS, AND PRAYERS FOR OTHERS ❧

{Dear Father, the temptation to try to build myself up at the expense of another is always available. Please keep me strong to side-step the temptation. I pray to remember that regardless of how disappointed I feel about the behavior of another, You have called me to pray for them and not to criticize them. Keep me prayerful today. Keep me in Your word so that I do not conform to behavior that is commonplace in the world around me. I pray these things in the name of Jesus. Amen.}

And rising very early in the morning, while it was still dark, he departed and went out to a desolate place, and there he prayed. ~ Mark 2:35

10. TODAY'S DATE_____

☐ Write down 1-3 issues that are presently dominating your thoughts and hindering your concentration. _____

*Legs aching, being tired
less concentration*

☐ Ask the Lord to move you away from these concerns, and to center your thoughts on Him. Ask to be filled with the Holy Spirit so that you hear and understand what God is saying in His word.

☐ On the line below, write your assignment for today (Or choose 3 new Bible chapters to read.)

_____

☐ Find an audio version of your reading assignment.

☐ While listening and reading, underline anything that catches your attention.

☐ Choose a verse, write down the address, and a few primary words from which will be your area of concentration.

☐ Journal on: (a) What comes to mind when reading over your Scripture selection, and/or (b) What might God be saying to you regarding your life and your issues in the light of these Scriptures?

☐ Write a prayer, and then pray it aloud to the Lord.

☐ If time allows, share your insights in a "Scripture, Thoughts, Prayer" format with others.

🌿 NOTES, PLANS, AND PRAYERS FOR OTHERS 🌿

{Dear Father, thank you for another day of having the opportunity to learn from Your word. I pray for the willingness and strength to have some quality time with You at the start of each day. Cause my heart to touch Your heart. Fill me with the remembrance that I am dearly loved and highly favored by You. You are my "Abba Father". I pray to not let the world's enticements or the devil's lies keep me from this special time with You. I pray in the name of Jesus. Amen.}

And he awoke and rebuked the wind and said to the sea, "Peace! Be still!" And the wind ceased, and there was a great calm. He said to them, "Why are you so afraid? Have you still no faith?" And they were filled with great fear and said to one another, "Who then is this, that even the wind and the sea obey him?"~ Mark 4:39-41

11. TODAY'S DATE_____

☐ Write down 1-3 issues that are presently dominating your thoughts and hindering your concentration. _____

_____
_____
_____
_____
_____
_____

☐ Ask the Lord to move you away from these concerns, and to center your thoughts on Him. Ask to be filled with the Holy Spirit so that you hear and understand what God is saying in His word.

☐ On the line below, write your assignment for today (Or choose 3 new Bible chapters to read.)

_____

☐ Find an audio version of your reading assignment.

☐ While listening and reading, underline anything that catches your attention.

☐ Choose a verse, write down the address, and a few primary words from which will be your area of concentration.

☐ Journal on: (a) What comes to mind when reading over your Scripture selection, and/or (b) What might God be saying to you regarding your life and your issues in the light of these Scriptures?

☐ Write a prayer, and then pray it aloud to the Lord.

☐ If time allows, share your insights in a "Scripture, Thoughts, Prayer" format with others.

🌿 NOTES, PLANS, AND PRAYERS FOR OTHERS 🌿

{Dear Father, thank you for teaching me not to censor my prayers. You can take the honest confessions of my thoughts and feelings. There is NOTHING that I cannot pray about. You love me. You listen to me. You show me time and time again how much You care for me. Thank you so, so much, Lord, for showing me this way to live. I want to stay deep in Your word today because I don't want anything hindering my ability to hear You. I don't want to miss the next miracle You have in store for me. I pray and give thanks in the name of Jesus Christ. Amen.}

Now there was no water for the congregation. And they assembled themselves together against Moses and against Aaron. And the people quarreled with Moses and said, "Would that we had perished when our brothers perished before the Lord! Why have you brought the assembly of the Lord into this wilderness, that we should die here, both we and our cattle? ~ Numbers 20:2-4

12. TODAY'S DATE_____

- ☐ Write down 1-3 issues that are presently dominating your thoughts and hindering your concentration. _____
_____
_____
_____
_____
_____

- ☐ Ask the Lord to move you away from these concerns, and to center your thoughts on Him. Ask to be filled with the Holy Spirit so that you hear and understand what God is saying in His word.

- ☐ On the line below, write your assignment for today (Or choose 3 new Bible chapters to read.)
_____

- ☐ Find an audio version of your reading assignment.

- ☐ While listening and reading, underline anything that catches your attention.

- ☐ Choose a verse, write down the address, and a few primary words from which will be your area of concentration.

- ☐ Journal on: (a) What comes to mind when reading over your Scripture selection, and/or (b) What might God be saying to you regarding your life and your issues in the light of these Scriptures?

- ☐ Write a prayer, and then pray it aloud to the Lord.

- ☐ If time allows, share your insights in a "Scripture, Thoughts, Prayer" format with others.

❈ NOTES, PLANS, AND PRAYERS FOR OTHERS ❈

{Dear Father, please do not let me be taken aback when people lash out in anger and bitterness. I pray to remember that EVERYBODY has flesh and every one of us has misbehaved in hurtful ways. In the midst of difficult encounters, please keep me coming to You so that I might continue to respond in wisdom, in truth, and in love. In the name of Jesus I pray. Amen.}

"And when he sits on the throne of his kingdom, he shall write for himself in a book a copy of this law, approved by the Levitical priests. And it shall be with him, and he shall read in it all the days of his life, that he may learn to fear the Lord his God by keeping all the words of this law and these statutes, and doing them, that his heart may not be lifted up above his brothers, and that he may not turn aside from the commandment, either to the right hand or to the left, so that he may continue long in his kingdom, he and his children, in Israel."
~ Deuteronomy 17:18-19

13. TODAY'S DATE_____

- ☐ Write down 1-3 issues that are presently dominating your thoughts and hindering your concentration. _____
_____
_____

- ☐ Ask the Lord to move you away from these concerns, and to center your thoughts on Him. Ask to be filled with the Holy Spirit so that you hear and understand what God is saying in His word.

- ☐ On the line below, write your assignment for today (Or choose 3 new Bible chapters to read.)
_____

- ☐ Find an audio version of your reading assignment.

- ☐ While listening and reading, underline anything that catches your attention.

- ☐ Choose a verse, write down the address, and a few primary words from which will be your area of concentration.

- ☐ Journal on: (a) What comes to mind when reading over your Scripture selection, and/or (b) What might God be saying to you regarding your life and your issues in the light of these Scriptures?

- ☐ Write a prayer, and then pray it aloud to the Lord.

- ☐ If time allows, share your insights in a "Scripture, Thoughts, Prayer" format with others.

🌿 NOTES, PLANS, AND PRAYERS FOR OTHERS 🌿

{Dear Father, You have opened my eyes to the busyness of the evil one. He is proclaiming his agenda and way of life on screens, in books, on radio, on billboards, in the mouths of others...you name it, he has his finger in the pot! Please, Lord, keep me diligent "not to conform to the pattern of this world, but to be transformed by the renewing of my mind" **(Romans 12:2)**. *Keep me purging my thinking of any rebellious thoughts. I pray to practice humility, to stay abstinent, and to prayerfully live out Your word today. I pray in the name of Jesus. Amen.}*

***But now, since you didn't believe what I said, you will be silent
and unable to speak until the child is born. For my words
will certainly be fulfilled at the proper time. ~ Luke 1:20***

14. TODAY'S DATE_____

- ☐ Write down 1-3 issues that are presently dominating your thoughts and hindering your concentration. _____
  _____
  _____
  _____
  _____
  _____
  _____

- ☐ Ask the Lord to move you away from these concerns, and to center your thoughts on Him. Ask to be filled with the Holy Spirit so that you hear and understand what God is saying in His word.

- ☐ On the line below, write your assignment for today (Or choose 3 new Bible chapters to read.)
  _____

- ☐ Find an audio version of your reading assignment.

- ☐ While listening and reading, underline anything that catches your attention.

- ☐ Choose a verse, write down the address, and a few primary words from which will be your area of concentration.

- ☐ Journal on: (a) What comes to mind when reading over your Scripture selection, and/or (b) What might God be saying to you regarding your life and your issues in the light of these Scriptures?

- ☐ Write a prayer, and then pray it aloud to the Lord.

- ☐ If time allows, share your insights in a "Scripture, Thoughts, Prayer" format with others.

🌿 NOTES, PLANS, AND PRAYERS FOR OTHERS 🌿

{Dear Father, please fill me with Your word so that I can sense the presence of untruth in my thinking. Teach me the language of the redeemed that will demolish all strongholds of unbelief. Please keep me vigilant to not let the devil use my mouth to sin. Keep me speaking the truth and encouraging others to do the same. Help us all to live courageously today— not knocked to the sidelines by habitual sin, nor bowled over by fear. It's in the mighty name of Jesus that I pray. Amen.}

"Put out into deep water, and let down the nets for a catch." Simon answered, "Master, we've worked hard all night and haven't caught anything. But because you say so, I will let down the nets." ~ Luke 5:4,5

15. TODAY'S DATE_____

- ☐ Write down 1-3 issues that are presently dominating your thoughts and hindering your concentration. _____
_____
_____
_____
_____
_____

- ☐ Ask the Lord to move you away from these concerns, and to center your thoughts on Him. Ask to be filled with the Holy Spirit so that you hear and understand what God is saying in His word.

- ☐ On the line below, write your assignment for today (Or choose 3 new Bible chapters to read.)
_____

- ☐ Find an audio version of your reading assignment.

- ☐ While listening and reading, underline anything that catches your attention.

- ☐ Choose a verse, write down the address, and a few primary words from which will be your area of concentration.

- ☐ Journal on: (a) What comes to mind when reading over your Scripture selection, and/or (b) What might God be saying to you regarding your life and your issues in the light of these Scriptures?

- ☐ Write a prayer, and then pray it aloud to the Lord.

- ☐ If time allows, share your insights in a "Scripture, Thoughts, Prayer" format with others.

❦ NOTES, PLANS, AND PRAYERS FOR OTHERS ❦

*{Dear Father, forgive me when I fear going out into deeper waters because of past failures. I pray to remember that You are the author of all that is truly good in my life. Give me courage to walk out in faith upon Your promises and revealed truth. I pray not to be haunted by my past, but to trust in You for a magnificent future. Keep me out of habitual sin. Keep me clear in my thinking. Keep me deep in Your word and knowing right from wrong. In You I am able to do immeasurably more that all I ask or imagine (**Ephesians 3:20**). Thank you for loving me so much! In Jesus' name I pray. Amen.}*

For the word of God is alive and active. Sharper than any double-edged sword, it penetrates even to dividing soul and spirit, joints and marrow; it judges the thoughts and attitudes of the heart. ~ Hebrews 4:12

 **16.** TODAY'S DATE_____

- ☐ Write down 1-3 issues that are presently dominating your thoughts and hindering your concentration. _____
_____
_____
_____
_____
_____

- ☐ Ask the Lord to move you away from these concerns, and to center your thoughts on Him. Ask to be filled with the Holy Spirit so that you hear and understand what God is saying in His word.

- ☐ On the line below, write your assignment for today (Or choose 3 new Bible chapters to read.)
_____

- ☐ Find an audio version of your reading assignment.

- ☐ While listening and reading, underline anything that catches your attention.

- ☐ Choose a verse, write down the address, and a few primary words from which will be your area of concentration.

- ☐ Journal on: (a) What comes to mind when reading over your Scripture selection, and/or (b) What might God be saying to you regarding your life and your issues in the light of these Scriptures?

- ☐ Write a prayer, and then pray it aloud to the Lord.

- ☐ If time allows, share your insights in a "Scripture, Thoughts, Prayer" format with others.

🌿 NOTES, PLANS, AND PRAYERS FOR OTHERS 🌿

{Dear Father, I pray to always stay immersed in Your word. Please keep me sitting at the feet of Jesus and drinking from the fount of living water. Keep me encouraging others to walk in this marvelous way. Please keep me abstinent so that my thinking is clear and I am not just merely "talking the talk". I pray in the holy name of Jesus. Amen.}

Finally, be strong in the Lord and in his great power. Put on the full armor of God so that you can fight against the devil's evil tricks. ~ Ephesians 6:10

17. TODAY'S DATE_____

- ☐ Write down 1-3 issues that are presently dominating your thoughts and hindering your concentration. _____
_____
_____
_____
_____
_____

- ☐ Ask the Lord to move you away from these concerns, and to center your thoughts on Him. Ask to be filled with the Holy Spirit so that you hear and understand what God is saying in His word.
- ☐ On the line below, write your assignment for today (Or choose 3 new Bible chapters to read.)
_____
- ☐ Find an audio version of your reading assignment.
- ☐ While listening and reading, underline anything that catches your attention.
- ☐ Choose a verse, write down the address, and a few primary words from which will be your area of concentration.
- ☐ Journal on: (a) What comes to mind when reading over your Scripture selection, and/or (b) What might God be saying to you regarding your life and your issues in the light of these Scriptures?
- ☐ Write a prayer, and then pray it aloud to the Lord.
- ☐ If time allows, share your insights in a "Scripture, Thoughts, Prayer" format with others.

🌿 NOTES, PLANS, AND PRAYERS FOR OTHERS 🌿

*{Dear Father, thank you for teaching me that my present suffering does not compare to the joy I am going to experience when Your glory is revealed (**1 Peter 4:12-13**). Nothing escapes You. You are all-knowing and You love me dearly. Keep me abstinent—No Matter What! Strengthen me to stand firm and to wait expectantly for the joy that You will reveal in this day. I pray in the name of Jesus. Amen.}*

Dear friends, do not believe every spirit, but test the spirits to see whether they are from God, because many false prophets have gone out into the world. This is how you can recognize the Spirit of God: Every spirit that acknowledges that Jesus Christ has come in the flesh is from God. ~ 1 John 4:1-2

18. TODAY'S DATE_____

- ☐ Write down 1-3 issues that are presently dominating your thoughts and hindering your concentration. _____
  _____
  _____
  _____
  _____
  _____
  _____

- ☐ Ask the Lord to move you away from these concerns, and to center your thoughts on Him. Ask to be filled with the Holy Spirit so that you hear and understand what God is saying in His word.

- ☐ On the line below, write your assignment for today (Or choose 3 new Bible chapters to read.)
  _____

- ☐ Find an audio version of your reading assignment.

- ☐ While listening and reading, underline anything that catches your attention.

- ☐ Choose a verse, write down the address, and a few primary words from which will be your area of concentration.

- ☐ Journal on: (a) What comes to mind when reading over your Scripture selection, and/or (b) What might God be saying to you regarding your life and your issues in the light of these Scriptures?

- ☐ Write a prayer, and then pray it aloud to the Lord.

- ☐ If time allows, share your insights in a "Scripture, Thoughts, Prayer" format with others.

🍂 NOTES, PLANS, AND PRAYERS FOR OTHERS 🌿

*{Dear Father, there are many places of learning, but only one source of truth. Your Son Jesus is the way, the truth, and the life (**John 14:6**). Thank you for teaching me that healing is more important than relief and only Jesus heals. Keep me wise and discerning regarding the friends and the fellowships I embrace. Keep me pointing others to Jesus. In His holy name I pray. Amen.}*

Depart from me, all you workers of evil, for the LORD has heard the sound of my weeping. ~ Psalm 6:8

19. TODAY'S DATE_____

- ☐ Write down 1-3 issues that are presently dominating your thoughts and hindering your concentration. _____
  _____
  _____
  _____
  _____
  _____

- ☐ Ask the Lord to move you away from these concerns, and to center your thoughts on Him. Ask to be filled with the Holy Spirit so that you hear and understand what God is saying in His word.

- ☐ On the line below, write your assignment for today (Or choose 3 new Bible chapters to read.)
  _____

- ☐ Find an audio version of your reading assignment.

- ☐ While listening and reading, underline anything that catches your attention.

- ☐ Choose a verse, write down the address, and a few primary words from which will be your area of concentration.

- ☐ Journal on: (a) What comes to mind when reading over your Scripture selection, and/or (b) What might God be saying to you regarding your life and your issues in the light of these Scriptures?

- ☐ Write a prayer, and then pray it aloud to the Lord.

- ☐ If time allows, share your insights in a "Scripture, Thoughts, Prayer" format with others.

🌿 NOTES, PLANS, AND PRAYERS FOR OTHERS 🌿

{Dear Father, for so many years the voices crushed every ounce of self-esteem that I could muster. I thank you, because this is not true today. I can live my life fearlessly today because I have a Savior. I don't have to run from life. I don't have to run to food or ANY false god today. You are my shield and my protector. I give thanks with praise in the name of Jesus Christ. Amen.}

If your brother sins against you, go and show him his fault, just between the two of you. If he listens to you, you have won your brother over. ~ Matthew 18:15

20. TODAY'S DATE_____

☐ Write down 1-3 issues that are presently dominating your thoughts and hindering your concentration. _____
_____
_____
_____
_____
_____
_____

☐ Ask the Lord to move you away from these concerns, and to center your thoughts on Him. Ask to be filled with the Holy Spirit so that you hear and understand what God is saying in His word.

☐ On the line below, write your assignment for today (Or choose 3 new Bible chapters to read.)
_____

☐ Find an audio version of your reading assignment.

☐ While listening and reading, underline anything that catches your attention.

☐ Choose a verse, write down the address, and a few primary words from which will be your area of concentration.

☐ Journal on: (a) What comes to mind when reading over your Scripture selection, and/or (b) What might God be saying to you regarding your life and your issues in the light of these Scriptures?

☐ Write a prayer, and then pray it aloud to the Lord.

☐ If time allows, share your insights in a "Scripture, Thoughts, Prayer" format with others.

✿ NOTES, PLANS, AND PRAYERS FOR OTHERS ✿

{Dear Father, thank you for New Life in the Spirit. Help me to watch and pray so that the devil cannot use me to hurt and destroy my brothers and sisters in Christ. Fill me with the love of Jesus so that I am a vital part of building Your church and not tearing it down. I pray to encourage my "siblings" to do the same. In the name of Jesus Christ I pray. Amen.}

> *"Of all the commandments, which is the most important?"*
> *"The most important one," answered Jesus, "is this: 'Hear, O Israel, the Lord our God, the Lord is one. Love the Lord your God with all your heart and with all your soul and with all your mind and with all your strength.* ~ Mark 12:28, 29

21. TODAY'S DATE_____

- ☐ Write down 1-3 issues that are presently dominating your thoughts and hindering your concentration. _____
  _____
  _____
  _____
  _____
  _____
  _____

- ☐ Ask the Lord to move you away from these concerns, and to center your thoughts on Him. Ask to be filled with the Holy Spirit so that you hear and understand what God is saying in His word.

- ☐ On the line below, write your assignment for today (Or choose 3 new Bible chapters to read.)
  _____

- ☐ Find an audio version of your reading assignment.

- ☐ While listening and reading, underline anything that catches your attention.

- ☐ Choose a verse, write down the address, and a few primary words from which will be your area of concentration.

- ☐ Journal on: (a) What comes to mind when reading over your Scripture selection, and/or (b) What might God be saying to you regarding your life and your issues in the light of these Scriptures?

- ☐ Write a prayer, and then pray it aloud to the Lord.

- ☐ If time allows, share your insights in a "Scripture, Thoughts, Prayer" format with others.

🌿 NOTES, PLANS, AND PRAYERS FOR OTHERS 🌿

{Dear Father, please forgive me for the many times when I have worried and fretted about things in this life. Help me to mature as a Christian and to trust You more. Grow me up so that I can make You proud for choosing me to be Your child. I am so very grateful for my salvation! I pray and give thanks in the name of Jesus Christ. Amen.}

***That they will come to their senses and escape from the trap
of the devil, who has taken them captive to do his will.***
~ 2 Timothy 2:26

22. TODAY'S DATE_____

- ☐ Write down 1-3 issues that are presently dominating your thoughts and hindering your concentration. _____
  _____
  _____
  _____
  _____
  _____
  _____

- ☐ Ask the Lord to move you away from these concerns, and to center your thoughts on Him. Ask to be filled with the Holy Spirit so that you hear and understand what God is saying in His word.

- ☐ On the line below, write your assignment for today (Or choose 3 new Bible chapters to read.)
  _____

- ☐ Find an audio version of your reading assignment.

- ☐ While listening and reading, underline anything that catches your attention.

- ☐ Choose a verse, write down the address, and a few primary words from which will be your area of concentration.

- ☐ Journal on: (a) What comes to mind when reading over your Scripture selection, and/or (b) What might God be saying to you regarding your life and your issues in the light of these Scriptures?

- ☐ Write a prayer, and then pray it aloud to the Lord.

- ☐ If time allows, share your insights in a "Scripture, Thoughts, Prayer" format with others.

❧ NOTES, PLANS, AND PRAYERS FOR OTHERS ❧

{Dear Father, thank you for showing me just how much time has been freed up by just getting my food in order. Thank you for my abstinence. You have given me a sanity and peace about food and eating that I would have never thought possible. Please keep me deep in Your word so that I am giving a clear and truthful message to all. I pray in the name of Jesus. Amen.}

The Spirit of the LORD is upon me, for he has anointed me to bring Good News to the poor. He has sent me to proclaim that captives will be released, that the blind will see, that the oppressed will be set free. ~ Luke 14:18

23. TODAY'S DATE_____

☐ Write down 1-3 issues that are presently dominating your thoughts and hindering your concentration. _____
_____
_____
_____
_____
_____
_____

☐ Ask the Lord to move you away from these concerns, and to center your thoughts on Him. Ask to be filled with the Holy Spirit so that you hear and understand what God is saying in His word.

☐ On the line below, write your assignment for today (Or choose 3 new Bible chapters to read.)
_____

☐ Find an audio version of your reading assignment.

☐ While listening and reading, underline anything that catches your attention.

☐ Choose a verse, write down the address, and a few primary words from which will be your area of concentration.

☐ Journal on: (a) What comes to mind when reading over your Scripture selection, and/or (b) What might God be saying to you regarding your life and your issues in the light of these Scriptures?

☐ Write a prayer, and then pray it aloud to the Lord.

☐ If time allows, share your insights in a "Scripture, Thoughts, Prayer" format with others.

🌿 NOTES, PLANS, AND PRAYERS FOR OTHERS 🌿

{Dear Father, You have given me my marching orders. I am to know You well so that I can effectively make You known. Please keep me out of the food. Please keep into Your word—drinking it in and living it out, each and every day. I pray to turn away from all thoughts, actions, and attitudes that compete with keeping You first place in my life. I pray in the name of Jesus. Amen.}

Our eyes look to the LORD our God, till he has mercy upon us. ~ Psalm 123:2

24. TODAY'S DATE_____

- ☐ Write down 1-3 issues that are presently dominating your thoughts and hindering your concentration. _____
  _____
  _____
  _____
  _____
  _____
  _____

- ☐ Ask the Lord to move you away from these concerns, and to center your thoughts on Him. Ask to be filled with the Holy Spirit so that you hear and understand what God is saying in His word.

- ☐ On the line below, write your assignment for today (Or choose 3 new Bible chapters to read.)
  _____

- ☐ Find an audio version of your reading assignment.

- ☐ While listening and reading, underline anything that catches your attention.

- ☐ Choose a verse, write down the address, and a few primary words from which will be your area of concentration.

- ☐ Journal on: (a) What comes to mind when reading over your Scripture selection, and/or (b) What might God be saying to you regarding your life and your issues in the light of these Scriptures?

- ☐ Write a prayer, and then pray it aloud to the Lord.

- ☐ If time allows, share your insights in a "Scripture, Thoughts, Prayer" format with others.

❧ NOTES, PLANS, AND PRAYERS FOR OTHERS ❧

{Dear Father, keep me in Your word today. Keep Your word in me so that I can know Your Truth. Thank you for reminding me that despite my feelings, I have much to be joyful about. I am saved. I am abstinent. I am loved by my creator and Lord. Thank you for keeping me. Thank you for being my shade in the scorching times of life—now and forevermore. I am Your servant and I pray to serve You well today and with gladness. I pray in the name of Jesus. Amen.}

Do not be overcome by evil, but overcome evil with good.
~ Romans 12:21

25. TODAY'S DATE_____

- ☐ Write down 1-3 issues that are presently dominating your thoughts and hindering your concentration. _____
  _____
  _____
  _____
  _____
  _____
  _____

- ☐ Ask the Lord to move you away from these concerns, and to center your thoughts on Him. Ask to be filled with the Holy Spirit so that you hear and understand what God is saying in His word.

- ☐ On the line below, write your assignment for today (Or choose 3 new Bible chapters to read.)
  _____

- ☐ Find an audio version of your reading assignment.

- ☐ While listening and reading, underline anything that catches your attention.

- ☐ Choose a verse, write down the address, and a few primary words from which will be your area of concentration.

- ☐ Journal on: (a) What comes to mind when reading over your Scripture selection, and/or (b) What might God be saying to you regarding your life and your issues in the light of these Scriptures?

- ☐ Write a prayer, and then pray it aloud to the Lord.

- ☐ If time allows, share your insights in a "Scripture, Thoughts, Prayer" format with others.

❦ NOTES, PLANS, AND PRAYERS FOR OTHERS ❦

{Dear Father, I pray to remember that You have called me to a life of supernatural love. Help me to remember that we all have flesh. Help me to remember that I have the Holy Spirit's power to rise above flesh. Keep me determined to live a joyful, giving and forgiving life. Keep me faithful in prayer and living harmoniously with others. Thank you for the blessing of this new life in Christ. I pray that in all I do others will sense the fervor and zeal that You have infused in me for You. I pray in the name of Jesus. Amen.}

Therefore, my dear brothers, stand firm. Let nothing move you. Always give yourselves fully to the work of the Lord, because you know that your labor in the Lord is not in vain.
~ 1 Corinthians 15:58

26. TODAY'S DATE_____

☐ Write down 1-3 issues that are presently dominating your thoughts and hindering your concentration. _____
_____
_____
_____
_____
_____
_____

☐ Ask the Lord to move you away from these concerns, and to center your thoughts on Him. Ask to be filled with the Holy Spirit so that you hear and understand what God is saying in His word.

☐ On the line below, write your assignment for today (Or choose 3 new Bible chapters to read.)
_____

☐ Find an audio version of your reading assignment.

☐ While listening and reading, underline anything that catches your attention.

☐ Choose a verse, write down the address, and a few primary words from which will be your area of concentration.

☐ Journal on: (a) What comes to mind when reading over your Scripture selection, and/or (b) What might God be saying to you regarding your life and your issues in the light of these Scriptures?

☐ Write a prayer, and then pray it aloud to the Lord.

☐ If time allows, share your insights in a "Scripture, Thoughts, Prayer" format with others.

🌿 NOTES, PLANS, AND PRAYERS FOR OTHERS 🌿

{Dear Father, please continue to strengthen me in this warzone called life. Please give me the willingness and the strength to spend quality time in Your word today. I pray to walk out boldly in the promises that You have made on my life. I pray in the name of Jesus. Amen.}

You will know the truth, and the truth will set you free.
~ John 8:32

27. TODAY'S DATE_____

- ☐ Write down 1-3 issues that are presently dominating your thoughts and hindering your concentration. _____
  _____
  _____
  _____
  _____
  _____
  _____

- ☐ Ask the Lord to move you away from these concerns, and to center your thoughts on Him. Ask to be filled with the Holy Spirit so that you hear and understand what God is saying in His word.

- ☐ On the line below, write your assignment for today (Or choose 3 new Bible chapters to read.)
  _____

- ☐ Find an audio version of your reading assignment.

- ☐ While listening and reading, underline anything that catches your attention.

- ☐ Choose a verse, write down the address, and a few primary words from which will be your area of concentration.

- ☐ Journal on: (a) What comes to mind when reading over your Scripture selection, and/or (b) What might God be saying to you regarding your life and your issues in the light of these Scriptures?

- ☐ Write a prayer, and then pray it aloud to the Lord.

- ☐ If time allows, share your insights in a "Scripture, Thoughts, Prayer" format with others.

❧ NOTES, PLANS, AND PRAYERS FOR OTHERS ❧

{Dear Father, keep us deep in Your word each day. Keep Your word deep in us. Keep us away from our known areas of sinful enticements. We want to know the truth. We want to remember Your anointing and the call that You have on our lives. You have set us free for freedom and we are eternally grateful! We pray and give thanks in the name of Jesus. Amen.}

***He must hold firmly to the trustworthy message as it has been
taught, so that he can encourage others by sound doctrine.
~ Titus 1:9***

28. TODAY'S DATE_____

- ☐ Write down 1-3 issues that are presently dominating your thoughts and hindering your concentration. _____
_____
_____
_____
_____
_____
_____

- ☐ Ask the Lord to move you away from these concerns, and to center your thoughts on Him. Ask to be filled with the Holy Spirit so that you hear and understand what God is saying in His word.

- ☐ On the line below, write your assignment for today (Or choose 3 new Bible chapters to read.)
_____

- ☐ Find an audio version of your reading assignment.

- ☐ While listening and reading, underline anything that catches your attention.

- ☐ Choose a verse, write down the address, and a few primary words from which will be your area of concentration.

- ☐ Journal on: (a) What comes to mind when reading over your Scripture selection, and/or (b) What might God be saying to you regarding your life and your issues in the light of these Scriptures?

- ☐ Write a prayer, and then pray it aloud to the Lord.

- ☐ If time allows, share your insights in a "Scripture, Thoughts, Prayer" format with others.

✣ NOTES, PLANS, AND PRAYERS FOR OTHERS ✣

{Dear Father, keep giving me the willingness and the strength to immerse myself in Your word each day. As You feed me with true food, You call me to turn to others and share with them Your empowering word. In giving truth to others, I sense Your presence even more and my blessings multiply! Thank you for loving me so dearly. I pray and give thanks in the name of Jesus. Amen.}

Blessed is the man who walks not in the counsel of the wicked, nor stands in the way of sinners, nor sits in the seat of scoffers. ~ Psalm 1:1

29. TODAY'S DATE _____

- ☐ Write down 1-3 issues that are presently dominating your thoughts and hindering your concentration. _____
_____
_____
_____
_____
_____
_____

- ☐ Ask the Lord to move you away from these concerns, and to center your thoughts on Him. Ask to be filled with the Holy Spirit so that you hear and understand what God is saying in His word.

- ☐ On the line below, write your assignment for today (Or choose 3 new Bible chapters to read.)
_____

- ☐ Find an audio version of your reading assignment.

- ☐ While listening and reading, underline anything that catches your attention.

- ☐ Choose a verse, write down the address, and a few primary words from which will be your area of concentration.

- ☐ Journal on: (a) What comes to mind when reading over your Scripture selection, and/or (b) What might God be saying to you regarding your life and your issues in the light of these Scriptures?

- ☐ Write a prayer, and then pray it aloud to the Lord.

- ☐ If time allows, share your insights in a "Scripture, Thoughts, Prayer" format with others.

🌿 NOTES, PLANS, AND PRAYERS FOR OTHERS 🌿

{Dear Father, You are teaching me that my mind is a powerful thing. I pray to stay alert—quick to dispel any thought that is not Godly and moving me toward a stronger life in Christ Jesus. The internet, magazines, newspapers and TV can affect me more than I can ever believe! I pray to guard my ears and my eyes at all times. I pray for those who are struggling with the food. I pray that they will honestly look at the amount of time that they spend under the counsel of the world as opposed to Your counsel in the Word. Please change their heart and open their eyes. Please continue to do the same for me. I pray this in the name of Jesus Christ. Amen.}

"Enter through the narrow gate; for the gate is wide and the way is broad that leads to destruction, and there are many who enter through it. For the gate is small and the way is narrow that leads to life, and there are few who find it.
~ Matthew 7:13-14

 30. TODAY'S DATE_____

- ☐ Write down 1-3 issues that are presently dominating your thoughts and hindering your concentration. _____
  _____
  _____
  _____
  _____
  _____
  _____

- ☐ Ask the Lord to move you away from these concerns, and to center your thoughts on Him. Ask to be filled with the Holy Spirit so that you hear and understand what God is saying in His word.

- ☐ On the line below, write your assignment for today (Or choose 3 new Bible chapters to read.)
  _____

- ☐ Find an audio version of your reading assignment.

- ☐ While listening and reading, underline anything that catches your attention.

- ☐ Choose a verse, write down the address, and a few primary words from which will be your area of concentration.

- ☐ Journal on: (a) What comes to mind when reading over your Scripture selection, and/or (b) What might God be saying to you regarding your life and your issues in the light of these Scriptures?

- ☐ Write a prayer, and then pray it aloud to the Lord.

- ☐ If time allows, share your insights in a "Scripture, Thoughts, Prayer" format with others.

❧ NOTES, PLANS, AND PRAYERS FOR OTHERS ❧

{Dear Father, may I never forget how lost and confused I was before I found Jesus. May I never stop caring for those who will perish if I fail to live Jesus out before them. Keep the narrow way before me. Keep me out of the food and immersed in Your word so that I keep maturing in my faith. Fill me up with your Holy Spirit so that I am not led astray by what I feel. Thank you, Jesus, for You never leave me or forsake me. I am Yours forever and the knowledge of this fills me with great joy! I pray and give thanks in Your holy name. Amen.}

He said, "Do not lay your hand on the boy or do anything to him, for now I know that you fear God, seeing you have not withheld your son, your only son, from me." ~ Genesis 22:12

 **31.** TODAY'S DATE_____

- ☐ Write down 1-3 issues that are presently dominating your thoughts and hindering your concentration. _____
_____
_____
_____
_____
_____
_____

- ☐ Ask the Lord to move you away from these concerns, and to center your thoughts on Him. Ask to be filled with the Holy Spirit so that you hear and understand what God is saying in His word.

- ☐ On the line below, write your assignment for today (Or choose 3 new Bible chapters to read.)
_____

- ☐ Find an audio version of your reading assignment.

- ☐ While listening and reading, underline anything that catches your attention.

- ☐ Choose a verse, write down the address, and a few primary words from which will be your area of concentration.

- ☐ Journal on: (a) What comes to mind when reading over your Scripture selection, and/or (b) What might God be saying to you regarding your life and your issues in the light of these Scriptures?

- ☐ Write a prayer, and then pray it aloud to the Lord.

- ☐ If time allows, share your insights in a "Scripture, Thoughts, Prayer" format with others.

🌿 NOTES, PLANS, AND PRAYERS FOR OTHERS 🌿

{Dear Father, thank you for another day to mature in faith. Please continue to grow me up. I hold on too tightly to what You provide, and in doing so, I forget about You. When I pray, help me to let go of whatever I am doing so that I can be surrendered heart-to-heart to You. Thank you for the many lessons of faith that You show me in Your word. Thank you for the "great cloud of witnesses" that spur me on by their examples of surrender. I am so grateful that I am not alone. I give thanks and pray in the name of Jesus. Amen.}

Open my eyes to see the wonderful truths in your instructions. I am only a foreigner in the land.
~ Psalm 119:18, 19

 32. TODAY'S DATE_____

- ☐ Write down 1-3 issues that are presently dominating your thoughts and hindering your concentration. _____
  _____
  _____
  _____
  _____
  _____
  _____

- ☐ Ask the Lord to move you away from these concerns, and to center your thoughts on Him. Ask to be filled with the Holy Spirit so that you hear and understand what God is saying in His word.

- ☐ On the line below, write your assignment for today (Or choose 3 new Bible chapters to read.)
  _____

- ☐ Find an audio version of your reading assignment.

- ☐ While listening and reading, underline anything that catches your attention.

- ☐ Choose a verse, write down the address, and a few primary words from which will be your area of concentration.

- ☐ Journal on: (a) What comes to mind when reading over your Scripture selection, and/or (b) What might God be saying to you regarding your life and your issues in the light of these Scriptures?

- ☐ Write a prayer, and then pray it aloud to the Lord.

- ☐ If time allows, share your insights in a "Scripture, Thoughts, Prayer" format with others.

❧ NOTES, PLANS, AND PRAYERS FOR OTHERS ❧

{Dear Father, what a delightful way to live. Despite the ups and downs of life, You have shown me how to stay joyful and full of Your peace. You have given me a purpose and a place. You are teaching me to know Your word and to live it out in the Spirit. This is the true, abundant life! Thank you for saving me and entrusting me to take this Good News out into the world today. Please keep me immersed in Your word. I pray in the name of Jesus. Amen.}

If you show favoritism, you sin. ~ James 2:9

33. TODAY'S DATE_____

☐ Write down 1-3 issues that are presently dominating your thoughts and hindering your concentration. _____

_____
_____
_____
_____
_____
_____

☐ Ask the Lord to move you away from these concerns, and to center your thoughts on Him. Ask to be filled with the Holy Spirit so that you hear and understand what God is saying in His word.

☐ On the line below, write your assignment for today (Or choose 3 new Bible chapters to read.)

_____

☐ Find an audio version of your reading assignment.

☐ While listening and reading, underline anything that catches your attention.

☐ Choose a verse, write down the address, and a few primary words from which will be your area of concentration.

☐ Journal on: (a) What comes to mind when reading over your Scripture selection, and/or (b) What might God be saying to you regarding your life and your issues in the light of these Scriptures?

☐ Write a prayer, and then pray it aloud to the Lord.

☐ If time allows, share your insights in a "Scripture, Thoughts, Prayer" format with others.

❧ NOTES, PLANS, AND PRAYERS FOR OTHERS ❧

{Dear Father, thank you for another day of learning from Your word. I pray to delight in all my children with equanimity! Convict me of my sin in this area. Please give me the willingness and the strength to amend my wrongs. May I keep Jesus before me as my divine model for life. Help me to see all people through His holy eyes of love. I pray in the name of Jesus Christ. Amen.}

You are my God; I shall seek You earnestly; My soul thirsts for You, my flesh yearns for You, In a dry and weary land where there is no water. ~ Psalm 63:1

34. TODAY'S DATE

- Write down 1-3 issues that are presently dominating your thoughts and hindering your concentration. _____
  _____
  _____
  _____
  _____
  _____
  _____

- Ask the Lord to move you away from these concerns, and to center your thoughts on Him. Ask to be filled with the Holy Spirit so that you hear and understand what God is saying in His word.

- On the line below, write your assignment for today (Or choose 3 new Bible chapters to read.)
  _____

- Find an audio version of your reading assignment.

- While listening and reading, underline anything that catches your attention.

- Choose a verse, write down the address, and a few primary words from which will be your area of concentration.

- Journal on: (a) What comes to mind when reading over your Scripture selection, and/or (b) What might God be saying to you regarding your life and your issues in the light of these Scriptures?

- Write a prayer, and then pray it aloud to the Lord.

- If time allows, share your insights in a "Scripture, Thoughts, Prayer" format with others.

❦ NOTES, PLANS, AND PRAYERS FOR OTHERS ❦

{Dear Father, thank you for teaching me that the willingness to be disciplined is a gift and not a hardship. May I keep Jesus before me in all that I do. May I seek to know Him and love Him better each day. May others come to be drawn to Jesus by sensing His presence in my life. In the name of Jesus I give thanks and pray. Amen.}

***Be on your guard against the yeast of the Pharisees
and Sadducees. ~ Matthew 16:11***

 **35.** TODAY'S DATE_____

☐ Write down 1-3 issues that are presently dominating your thoughts and hindering your concentration. _____
_____
_____
_____
_____
_____

☐ Ask the Lord to move you away from these concerns, and to center your thoughts on Him. Ask to be filled with the Holy Spirit so that you hear and understand what God is saying in His word.

☐ On the line below, write your assignment for today (Or choose 3 new Bible chapters to read.)
_____

☐ Find an audio version of your reading assignment.

☐ While listening and reading, underline anything that catches your attention.

☐ Choose a verse, write down the address, and a few primary words from which will be your area of concentration.

☐ Journal on: (a) What comes to mind when reading over your Scripture selection, and/or (b) What might God be saying to you regarding your life and your issues in the light of these Scriptures?

☐ Write a prayer, and then pray it aloud to the Lord.

☐ If time allows, share your insights in a "Scripture, Thoughts, Prayer" format with others.

🌿 NOTES, PLANS, AND PRAYERS FOR OTHERS 🌿

{Dear Father, thank you for another day of abstinence and learning from Your word. You are showing me that the devil is busy and his tactics are sneaky. Help me to remember that I cannot mindlessly take in evil and think that I will be unaffected. Please fill me with Your truth so that I can keep a guard against those "delightful" things that poison my heart and steal my time. When I am tempted, please give me the willingness and strength, to pray for willingness and strength! It's in the name of the Lord Jesus Christ that I pray. Amen.}

And the people of Israel again did what was evil in the sight of the LORD. ~ *Judges 13:1*

 **36.** TODAY'S DATE_____

- ☐ Write down 1-3 issues that are presently dominating your thoughts and hindering your concentration. _____
  _____
  _____
  _____
  _____
  _____

- ☐ Ask the Lord to move you away from these concerns, and to center your thoughts on Him. Ask to be filled with the Holy Spirit so that you hear and understand what God is saying in His word.

- ☐ On the line below, write your assignment for today (Or choose 3 new Bible chapters to read.)
  _____

- ☐ Find an audio version of your reading assignment.

- ☐ While listening and reading, underline anything that catches your attention.

- ☐ Choose a verse, write down the address, and a few primary words from which will be your area of concentration.

- ☐ Journal on: (a) What comes to mind when reading over your Scripture selection, and/or (b) What might God be saying to you regarding your life and your issues in the light of these Scriptures?

- ☐ Write a prayer, and then pray it aloud to the Lord.

- ☐ If time allows, share your insights in a "Scripture, Thoughts, Prayer" format with others.

❧ NOTES, PLANS, AND PRAYERS FOR OTHERS ❧

{Dear Father, I pray that I have learned my lesson for the rest of my life. Your love can never be forgotten. Neither can it be taken for granted. You are love and the greatness of this love can never take second place to anything! I pray to dig deeply into Your word today so that I can know You better and to love You more. I pray to turn away from all my idols, especially the grand idol of my past—overeating. Your love has transformed me. I trust in Your love. I rejoice in Your love. In the name of Jesus I give thanks and praise. Amen.}

"You are the light of the world. A city set on a hill cannot be hidden; nor does anyone light a lamp and put it under a basket, but on the lamp stand, and it gives light to all who are in the house. ~ Matthew 5:14-15

37. TODAY'S DATE _____

☐ Write down 1-3 issues that are presently dominating your thoughts and hindering your concentration. _____
_____
_____
_____
_____
_____
_____

☐ Ask the Lord to move you away from these concerns, and to center your thoughts on Him. Ask to be filled with the Holy Spirit so that you hear and understand what God is saying in His word.

☐ On the line below, write your assignment for today (Or choose 3 new Bible chapters to read.)
_____

☐ Find an audio version of your reading assignment.

☐ While listening and reading, underline anything that catches your attention.

☐ Choose a verse, write down the address, and a few primary words from which will be your area of concentration.

☐ Journal on: (a) What comes to mind when reading over your Scripture selection, and/or (b) What might God be saying to you regarding your life and your issues in the light of these Scriptures?

☐ Write a prayer, and then pray it aloud to the Lord.

☐ If time allows, share your insights in a "Scripture, Thoughts, Prayer" format with others.

❧ NOTES, PLANS, AND PRAYERS FOR OTHERS ❧

{Dear Father, thank you for showing me how compulsive overeating was destroying my life. Thank you for showing me how delightful it is to have deep fellowship with You through Bible Immersion. I pray to remember that You have kingdom work for me to do each and every day. Nothing is more important than living my life in a way that points others to Jesus. Please show me the areas in my life where I allow my flesh to be in control. I pray for the willingness and the strength to turn away from these dark places. It's in the name of Jesus that I pray. Amen.}

For we are God's handiwork, created in Christ Jesus to do good works, which God prepared in advance for us to do.
~ Ephesians 2:10

 **38.** TODAY'S DATE_____

☐ Write down 1-3 issues that are presently dominating your thoughts and hindering your concentration. _____
_____
_____
_____
_____
_____

☐ Ask the Lord to move you away from these concerns, and to center your thoughts on Him. Ask to be filled with the Holy Spirit so that you hear and understand what God is saying in His word.

☐ On the line below, write your assignment for today (Or choose 3 new Bible chapters to read.)
_____

☐ Find an audio version of your reading assignment.

☐ While listening and reading, underline anything that catches your attention.

☐ Choose a verse, write down the address, and a few primary words from which will be your area of concentration.

☐ Journal on: (a) What comes to mind when reading over your Scripture selection, and/or (b) What might God be saying to you regarding your life and your issues in the light of these Scriptures?

☐ Write a prayer, and then pray it aloud to the Lord.

☐ If time allows, share your insights in a "Scripture, Thoughts, Prayer" format with others.

✿ NOTES, PLANS, AND PRAYERS FOR OTHERS ✿

{Dear Father, please keep me focused on Jesus and moving beyond my flesh. Open my eyes to the good work that You have planned for me to do today. Thank you for all that You are teaching me about life and living through Your word, the Bible. Please keep me abstinent and living in the freedom to fuel my body without slowing it down. I give thanks and praise in the name of Jesus Christ. Amen.}

He had seven hundred wives of royal birth and three hundred concubines, and his wives led him astray. As Solomon grew old, his wives turned his heart after other gods.
~ 1 Kings 11:3-4

39. TODAY'S DATE_____

- ☐ Write down 1-3 issues that are presently dominating your thoughts and hindering your concentration. _____
  _____
  _____
  _____
  _____
  _____
  _____

- ☐ Ask the Lord to move you away from these concerns, and to center your thoughts on Him. Ask to be filled with the Holy Spirit so that you hear and understand what God is saying in His word.

- ☐ On the line below, write your assignment for today (Or choose 3 new Bible chapters to read.)
  _____

- ☐ Find an audio version of your reading assignment.

- ☐ While listening and reading, underline anything that catches your attention.

- ☐ Choose a verse, write down the address, and a few primary words from which will be your area of concentration.

- ☐ Journal on: (a) What comes to mind when reading over your Scripture selection, and/or (b) What might God be saying to you regarding your life and your issues in the light of these Scriptures?

- ☐ Write a prayer, and then pray it aloud to the Lord.

- ☐ If time allows, share your insights in a "Scripture, Thoughts, Prayer" format with others.

🌿 NOTES, PLANS, AND PRAYERS FOR OTHERS 🌿

*{Dear Father, thank you for another day of growing in truth through Your word. Help me to learn from the ones who have lived before me. I pray to remember that I have a choice—I can choose to walk in Christ's footsteps or to walk in the flesh. I pray to make the choice for Jesus early and often each day. When I keep Jesus first and center, He shows me the pitfalls, the minefields, and the clear path to an abundantly rich life. Thank you, Father, for loving me so dearly and showing the way. Thank you that even when I am not willing, You can give me the willingness to be willing (**Philippians 2:13**). I pray for this today. May I keep You at the center in every season of my life! In the name of Jesus I pray. Amen.}*

*Do everything without complaining or arguing, so that you
may become blameless and pure, children of God without fault
in a crooked and depraved generation, in which you shine
like stars in the universe as you hold out the word of life.*
~ Philippians 2:14-16

 # 40. TODAY'S DATE_____

- ☐ Write down 1-3 issues that are presently dominating your thoughts and hindering your concentration. _____
  _____
  _____
  _____
  _____
  _____
  _____

- ☐ Ask the Lord to move you away from these concerns, and to center your thoughts on Him. Ask to be filled with the Holy Spirit so that you hear and understand what God is saying in His word.

- ☐ On the line below, write your assignment for today (Or choose 3 new Bible chapters to read.)
  _____

- ☐ Find an audio version of your reading assignment.

- ☐ While listening and reading, underline anything that catches your attention.

- ☐ Choose a verse, write down the address, and a few primary words from which will be your area of concentration.

- ☐ Journal on: (a) What comes to mind when reading over your Scripture selection, and/or (b) What might God be saying to you regarding your life and your issues in the light of these Scriptures?

- ☐ Write a prayer, and then pray it aloud to the Lord.

- ☐ If time allows, share your insights in a "Scripture, Thoughts, Prayer" format with others.

❦ NOTES, PLANS, AND PRAYERS FOR OTHERS ❦

{Dear Father, I pray to never forget that Jesus went through much pain for my freedom. I pray that when I am visited by painful times, that I will keep free from murmuring and complaining. Living in this world is not trouble-free, but each day can be joy-filled and beautiful. I pray to let Your word transform me. I pray to cooperate by yielding to Your program of selfless behavior in the power of the Spirit. It's in the name of Jesus that I pray. Amen.}

So I say, let the Holy Spirit guide your lives. Then you won't be doing what your sinful nature craves. ~ Galatians 5:16

41. TODAY'S DATE_____

- ☐ Write down 1-3 issues that are presently dominating your thoughts and hindering your concentration. _____
  _____
  _____
  _____
  _____
  _____
  _____

- ☐ Ask the Lord to move you away from these concerns, and to center your thoughts on Him. Ask to be filled with the Holy Spirit so that you hear and understand what God is saying in His word.

- ☐ On the line below, write your assignment for today (Or choose 3 new Bible chapters to read.)
  _____

- ☐ Find an audio version of your reading assignment.

- ☐ While listening and reading, underline anything that catches your attention.

- ☐ Choose a verse, write down the address, and a few primary words from which will be your area of concentration.

- ☐ Journal on: (a) What comes to mind when reading over your Scripture selection, and/or (b) What might God be saying to you regarding your life and your issues in the light of these Scriptures?

- ☐ Write a prayer, and then pray it aloud to the Lord.

- ☐ If time allows, share your insights in a "Scripture, Thoughts, Prayer" format with others.

🌿 NOTES, PLANS, AND PRAYERS FOR OTHERS 🌿

{Dear Father, I pray to share clearly and truthfully the things You are teaching me. I pray to keep practicing Your lessons and making them my own. Please keep me out of the food. Please keep me deep in Your word so that my sword is ready for the next attack. It is in the name of Jesus that I pray. Amen.}

No one else so completely sold himself to what was evil in the Lord's sight as Ahab did under the influence of his wife Jezebel. ~ 1 Kings 21:25

42. TODAY'S DATE_____

☐ Write down 1-3 issues that are presently dominating your thoughts and hindering your concentration. _____
_____
_____
_____
_____
_____
_____

☐ Ask the Lord to move you away from these concerns, and to center your thoughts on Him. Ask to be filled with the Holy Spirit so that you hear and understand what God is saying in His word.

☐ On the line below, write your assignment for today (Or choose 3 new Bible chapters to read.)

_____

☐ Find an audio version of your reading assignment.

☐ While listening and reading, underline anything that catches your attention.

☐ Choose a verse, write down the address, and a few primary words from which will be your area of concentration.

☐ Journal on: (a) What comes to mind when reading over your Scripture selection, and/or (b) What might God be saying to you regarding your life and your issues in the light of these Scriptures?

☐ Write a prayer, and then pray it aloud to the Lord.

☐ If time allows, share your insights in a "Scripture, Thoughts, Prayer" format with others.

🌿 NOTES, PLANS, AND PRAYERS FOR OTHERS 🌿

*{Dear Father, I pray to remember that I have a choice to either walk with the Spirit or to let the flesh be in control. I pray to live like a child of The Light today (**Philippians 2:14-16**). I pray to be like Jesus. Please help me to take the time to hear You speak to my heart through Your word today. I pray for a filling of the Holy Spirit so that I am empowered to do the things that You have asked me to do. Please keep me abstinent and running to You and not to false idols today. Help me to learn a lesson from those who have failed before me. I pray in the name of Jesus Christ. Amen.}*

"You search the Scriptures, for you believe they give you eternal life. And the Scriptures point to me! Yet you won't come to me so that I can give you this life eternal!
~ John 5:39-40

43. TODAY'S DATE_____

- ☐ Write down 1-3 issues that are presently dominating your thoughts and hindering your concentration. _____
_____
_____
_____
_____
_____

- ☐ Ask the Lord to move you away from these concerns, and to center your thoughts on Him. Ask to be filled with the Holy Spirit so that you hear and understand what God is saying in His word.

- ☐ On the line below, write your assignment for today (Or choose 3 new Bible chapters to read.)
_____

- ☐ Find an audio version of your reading assignment.

- ☐ While listening and reading, underline anything that catches your attention.

- ☐ Choose a verse, write down the address, and a few primary words from which will be your area of concentration.

- ☐ Journal on: (a) What comes to mind when reading over your Scripture selection, and/or (b) What might God be saying to you regarding your life and your issues in the light of these Scriptures?

- ☐ Write a prayer, and then pray it aloud to the Lord.

- ☐ If time allows, share your insights in a "Scripture, Thoughts, Prayer" format with others.

❧ NOTES, PLANS, AND PRAYERS FOR OTHERS ❧

{Dear Father, this is the day that you have made and have given to me. I pray to prize You above all other people, places, and things. You have taught me that when I truly put You first in my day, I don't have to worry about my food or anything else. I pray to continue to bring my thoughts to You. I pray to teach this to others with all the love and skill that You can give me. I pray in the name of Jesus. Amen.}

God opposes the proud but shows favor to the humble.
~ James 4:6

44. TODAY'S DATE_____

- ☐ Write down 1-3 issues that are presently dominating your thoughts and hindering your concentration. _____
  _____
  _____
  _____
  _____
  _____
  _____

- ☐ Ask the Lord to move you away from these concerns, and to center your thoughts on Him. Ask to be filled with the Holy Spirit so that you hear and understand what God is saying in His word.

- ☐ On the line below, write your assignment for today (Or choose 3 new Bible chapters to read.)
  _____

- ☐ Find an audio version of your reading assignment.

- ☐ While listening and reading, underline anything that catches your attention.

- ☐ Choose a verse, write down the address, and a few primary words from which will be your area of concentration.

- ☐ Journal on: (a) What comes to mind when reading over your Scripture selection, and/or (b) What might God be saying to you regarding your life and your issues in the light of these Scriptures?

- ☐ Write a prayer, and then pray it aloud to the Lord.

- ☐ If time allows, share your insights in a "Scripture, Thoughts, Prayer" format with others.

🌿 NOTES, PLANS, AND PRAYERS FOR OTHERS 🌿

{Dear Father, thank you for another day of abstinence and living in the word. Even when I was young I was in the crosshairs of the devil's weapons of annihilation. Thank you for sending Jesus to save me. You are teaching me how to live this life victoriously—not tethered to anyone except the Lord. Please keep me forever abiding in the Lord. I pray to teach others to do the same. It is in the name of Jesus Christ that I pray. Amen.}

Search me, God, and know my heart; test me and know my anxious thoughts. See if there is any offensive way in me, and lead me in the way everlasting. ~ Psalm 139:23-24

 **45.** TODAY'S DATE_____

- ☐ Write down 1-3 issues that are presently dominating your thoughts and hindering your concentration. _____
  _____
  _____
  _____
  _____
  _____
  _____

- ☐ Ask the Lord to move you away from these concerns, and to center your thoughts on Him. Ask to be filled with the Holy Spirit so that you hear and understand what God is saying in His word.

- ☐ On the line below, write your assignment for today (Or choose 3 new Bible chapters to read.)
  _____

- ☐ Find an audio version of your reading assignment.

- ☐ While listening and reading, underline anything that catches your attention.

- ☐ Choose a verse, write down the address, and a few primary words from which will be your area of concentration.

- ☐ Journal on: (a) What comes to mind when reading over your Scripture selection, and/or (b) What might God be saying to you regarding your life and your issues in the light of these Scriptures?

- ☐ Write a prayer, and then pray it aloud to the Lord.

- ☐ If time allows, share your insights in a "Scripture, Thoughts, Prayer" format with others.

❦ NOTES, PLANS, AND PRAYERS FOR OTHERS ❦

*{Dear Father, You have taught me that I have often missed out on Your blessings because I have failed to ask You for what I've needed (**James 4:2**). I pray to remember that nothing is impossible for You. You can change me into the likeness of your Son. Help me to keep a close watch on myself and on Your teachings. Please grow my faith and fill me with sober judgement. Keep me from being stunted in my growth by overwhelming emotional strife. Please keep me out of the food and into Your word. I pray in the name of Jesus Christ, my Savior and my Lord. Amen.}*

I took you from the pasture, from following the sheep, to be prince over my people Israel. ~ 1 Chronicles 17:7

46. TODAY'S DATE_____

- [ ] Write down 1-3 issues that are presently dominating your thoughts and hindering your concentration. _____
  _____
  _____
  _____
  _____
  _____

- [ ] Ask the Lord to move you away from these concerns, and to center your thoughts on Him. Ask to be filled with the Holy Spirit so that you hear and understand what God is saying in His word.

- [ ] On the line below, write your assignment for today (Or choose 3 new Bible chapters to read.)
  _____

- [ ] Find an audio version of your reading assignment.

- [ ] While listening and reading, underline anything that catches your attention.

- [ ] Choose a verse, write down the address, and a few primary words from which will be your area of concentration.

- [ ] Journal on: (a) What comes to mind when reading over your Scripture selection, and/or (b) What might God be saying to you regarding your life and your issues in the light of these Scriptures?

- [ ] Write a prayer, and then pray it aloud to the Lord.

- [ ] If time allows, share your insights in a "Scripture, Thoughts, Prayer" format with others.

❧ NOTES, PLANS, AND PRAYERS FOR OTHERS ❧

{Dear Father, You have plans for my life and You know what they are. Keep me humbly coming before You throughout the day asking for the next right thing to do. Help me to stay the right size. Before I attempt to do for You, I pray to remember what You have done for me. Your love for me is amazing! I pray that my abstinent life today in the word, will bring honor to You. It is in the name of Jesus that I pray. Amen.}

Anyone who belongs to Christ has become a new person. The old life is gone; a new life has begun! And all of this is a gift from God, who brought us back to himself through Christ. And God has given us this task of reconciling people to him.
~ 2 Corinthians 5:17-18

 47. TODAY'S DATE_____

- ☐ Write down 1-3 issues that are presently dominating your thoughts and hindering your concentration. _____
_____

- ☐ Ask the Lord to move you away from these concerns, and to center your thoughts on Him. Ask to be filled with the Holy Spirit so that you hear and understand what God is saying in His word.

- ☐ On the line below, write your assignment for today (Or choose 3 new Bible chapters to read.)
_____

- ☐ Find an audio version of your reading assignment.

- ☐ While listening and reading, underline anything that catches your attention.

- ☐ Choose a verse, write down the address, and a few primary words from which will be your area of concentration.

- ☐ Journal on: (a) What comes to mind when reading over your Scripture selection, and/or (b) What might God be saying to you regarding your life and your issues in the light of these Scriptures?

- ☐ Write a prayer, and then pray it aloud to the Lord.

- ☐ If time allows, share your insights in a "Scripture, Thoughts, Prayer" format with others.

🌿 NOTES, PLANS, AND PRAYERS FOR OTHERS 🌿

{Dear Father, Your word the Bible is magnificent! Why would I want to keep pursuing any counsel other than Your inerrant word! There is so much to learn. There is so much that You want to teach me. Thank you for giving me a passion to learn from Scripture today. Thank you that I know that the Bible keeps me eye to eye with Jesus and Your will for my life today. May I never forget for one moment that Your will for this day DOES NOT include lusting after food! Please keep me learning and growing through Bible Immersion. Please keep me encouraging others to do the same. It is in the name of Jesus that I pray. Amen.}

For the word of God is alive and powerful. It is sharper than the sharpest two-edged sword, cutting between soul and spirit, between joint and marrow. It exposes our innermost thoughts and desires. ~ Hebrews 4:12

48. TODAY'S DATE_____

☐ Write down 1-3 issues that are presently dominating your thoughts and hindering your concentration. _____
_____
_____
_____
_____
_____

☐ Ask the Lord to move you away from these concerns, and to center your thoughts on Him. Ask to be filled with the Holy Spirit so that you hear and understand what God is saying in His word.

☐ On the line below, write your assignment for today (Or choose 3 new Bible chapters to read.)
_____

☐ Find an audio version of your reading assignment.

☐ While listening and reading, underline anything that catches your attention.

☐ Choose a verse, write down the address, and a few primary words from which will be your area of concentration.

☐ Journal on: (a) What comes to mind when reading over your Scripture selection, and/or (b) What might God be saying to you regarding your life and your issues in the light of these Scriptures?

☐ Write a prayer, and then pray it aloud to the Lord.

☐ If time allows, share your insights in a "Scripture, Thoughts, Prayer" format with others.

❧ NOTES, PLANS, AND PRAYERS FOR OTHERS ❧

_____
_____
_____
_____
_____
_____
_____
_____
_____
_____
_____
_____
_____
_____
_____
_____
_____
_____
_____
_____
_____
_____
_____
_____
_____
_____
_____

*{Dear Father, thank you for the willingness to put meeting with You at the top of this day. Please help me to remember that my thoughts will influence my attitudes and feelings. Keep me running to Your word today when I feel off and overwhelmed. Keep me digging deeper and praying about the insights that You reveal, as I pursue You in this way. Thank you, Lord, because being immersed in Your word has given me a special added bonus. Your word has become hands-down, better than any food that I have ever known! You are showing me the path of life (**Psalm 16:11**). I pray to stay rooted in Your word forever. It is in the name of Jesus Christ that I pray. Amen.}*

He set to work resolutely and built up all the wall that was broken down and raised towers upon it, and outside it he built another wall, and he strengthened the Millo in the city of David. He also made weapons and shields in abundance.
~ 2 Chronicles 32:5

49. TODAY'S DATE _____

- ☐ Write down 1-3 issues that are presently dominating your thoughts and hindering your concentration. _____
_____
_____
_____
_____
_____
_____

- ☐ Ask the Lord to move you away from these concerns, and to center your thoughts on Him. Ask to be filled with the Holy Spirit so that you hear and understand what God is saying in His word.

- ☐ On the line below, write your assignment for today (Or choose 3 new Bible chapters to read.)
_____

- ☐ Find an audio version of your reading assignment.

- ☐ While listening and reading, underline anything that catches your attention.

- ☐ Choose a verse, write down the address, and a few primary words from which will be your area of concentration.

- ☐ Journal on: (a) What comes to mind when reading over your Scripture selection, and/or (b) What might God be saying to you regarding your life and your issues in the light of these Scriptures?

- ☐ Write a prayer, and then pray it aloud to the Lord.

- ☐ If time allows, share your insights in a "Scripture, Thoughts, Prayer" format with others.

🌿 NOTES, PLANS, AND PRAYERS FOR OTHERS 🌿

*{Dear Father, thank you for another day of abstinence and being immersed in Your word. Please help me to remember that I have been reborn and that You have not given me a spirit of fear, but a spirit of power and love and of self-discipline (**2 Timothy 1:7**). Give me the courage to stand firm in my faith. Keep me prayerful and trusting that at the exact right time You will supply all that I need for success—including affirmation and reward. You want the best for me and doing life Your way is always the best. It's in the name of Jesus I pray. Amen.}*

He said: "Listen, King Jehoshaphat and all who live in Judah and Jerusalem! This is what the LORD says to you: 'Do not be afraid or discouraged because of this vast army. For the battle is not yours, but God's. ~ 2 Chronicles 20:15

50. TODAY'S DATE_____

☐ Write down 1-3 issues that are presently dominating your thoughts and hindering your concentration. _____
_____
_____
_____
_____
_____
_____

☐ Ask the Lord to move you away from these concerns, and to center your thoughts on Him. Ask to be filled with the Holy Spirit so that you hear and understand what God is saying in His word.

☐ On the line below, write your assignment for today (Or choose 3 new Bible chapters to read.)
_____

☐ Find an audio version of your reading assignment.

☐ While listening and reading, underline anything that catches your attention.

☐ Choose a verse, write down the address, and a few primary words from which will be your area of concentration.

☐ Journal on: (a) What comes to mind when reading over your Scripture selection, and/or (b) What might God be saying to you regarding your life and your issues in the light of these Scriptures?

☐ Write a prayer, and then pray it aloud to the Lord.

☐ If time allows, share your insights in a "Scripture, Thoughts, Prayer" format with others.

❧ NOTES, PLANS, AND PRAYERS FOR OTHERS ❧

{Dear Father, I pray to remember Your anointing and Your call on my life. There are captives that need to be set free. There are blind ones who are crying out to see again. There is a world around me that is perishing for lack of knowing the Good News of Jesus Christ. Bring back to my mind the lessons You have taught me in Your word. Fill me with the Holy Spirit so that I can rise above my feelings and walk out boldly in Your truth. In Jesus' name. Amen.}

Readings to Help You Stay on Course

1.

READING THROUGH THE BIBLE EACH YEAR

These things happened to them as an example, but they were written down for our instruction, on whom the end of the ages has come. ~ 1 Corinthians 10:11

Before going any further, it is important that you understand the key component that makes Bible Immersion "work". **Bible Immersion requires that the student reads through the entire Bible every year**. It is not a "read the Bible one weekend" deal that is being asked. Nor is it a "read the Bible in so many days" affair. The strong statement that Bible Immersion is making is that reading through the Bible, year after year, needs to become a life-long discipline. If a Christian is over the age of 21, and is not mentally challenged, this is not only doable (15-20 minutes per day) it is CRUCIAL!

Each day we move closer to the return of Jesus. The Bible has told us that these days will be filled with an increasing amount of blatant sinfulness! *There will be terrible times in the last days. People will be lovers of themselves, lovers of money, boastful, proud, abusive, disobedient to their parents, ungrateful, unholy, without love, unforgiving, slanderous, without self-control, brutal, not lovers of the good, treacherous, rash, conceited, lovers of pleasure rather than lovers of God—having a form of godliness but denying its power. (2 Timothy 3:1-5)* **NIV**

Additionally there will be a proliferation of false teachers. They and the lies they tell will be so cleverly dressed up that they will give the appearance of truth. Without an on-going knowledge of what God says in His word we could be easily swayed by what sounds Biblical, yet is nowhere to be found in the pages of Scripture!

In Bible Immersion it is recommended that a student reads about 3 chapters of Scripture each day. This will not only move them along to complete the Bible-in-a-year goal, it will also serve to reset the thinking of the student. The word of God has a cleansing capability. As we live in the world we get influenced by the things of the world. The world has an agenda that runs counter to the things of God. By the end of the day each person has received training in how to live in the flesh. We have been shown how to speak it, and how to act it out. The decision to counter-act this barrage must be purposeful. When any amount of the word is given it can do remarkable things. But when a substantial amount of the word is introduced into a life daily, the student himself begins to notice.

If you have not begun moving toward the commitment to read through the Bible each year, please take the time right now to pray for the willingness and the strength to do this. Remember that there is a reading schedule found at the end of this book. Ask the Lord frequently for the willingness and the strength to stay deep in His word daily, and for a lifetime!

*{Dear Father, one day Jesus will come back to take me to be where He is (**John 14: 3**). As I wait His return, I pray to live a life that pleases You. Please keep me immersed in Your word each day. Please keep me trained and equipped—teaching others to do the same. In the name of Jesus I pray. Amen.}*

2.

PRAY WITHOUT CEASING

Be anxious for nothing, but in everything by prayer and supplication with thanksgiving let your requests be made known to God. And the peace of God, which surpasses all comprehension, will guard your hearts and your minds in Christ Jesus. ~ Philippians 4:6

The Bible tells us that we are to pray without ceasing (***1 Thessalonians 5:17***). This is particularly important when we are doing Bible Immersion. Keep in mind that Bible Immersion is going to engage both your mind and your heart. You are going to witness God's direct care and intervention in your life.

There is always a lot of resistance to anyone interacting with the word of God in a deep and meaningful way. It would be foolish to not expect opposition when engaged in Bible Immersion. It would be even more foolish not to prepare myself! My preparation is prayer, prayer, and more prayer. I pray before starting Bible Immersion. I pray while I am engaged in Bible Immersion. I end my Bible Immersion time with both a written and spoken prayer.

I have established a routine. When I get out of bed in the morning, I find a quiet place to kneel and I pray to the Lord from my heart. In fact, on most mornings I purpose to pray even before I get down on my knees. On these days, as soon as I open my eyes I start whispering to the Lord. I speak to Him as He is— the closest friend I have. Through Bible Immersion I have experienced that His love for me is deep and never ending. I want Him to know how grateful I am to be His.

I then spend about five minutes on my knees. While kneeling, there are some ongoing things that I thank the Lord for and some ongoing things that I petition Him about. I follow these with some new "thanksgivings" and new supplications. While involved in grooming I have learned to prep my mind for the study to follow, by listening to the passages that I will be reading. From here I move to my desk to begin a time in Bible Immersion.

I have discovered that prayer is how I talk to God and Bible Immersion is how I hear from Him. Since I have a history of hearing many voices in my head that often masquerade as truth, I cry out to God to safeguard my mind. I do not want to be fooled and living in self-denial. I ask the Father to fill me up with the Holy Spirit so that I can hear and understand what God is saying to me in His word. I know that He will answer this petition because the Bible has assured me that He will!

In the Bible I remember learning that on the night before the crucifixion, Jesus told the apostles that He was going to ask His Father to send a helper to them. This helper is the Holy Spirit. He teaches us and He reminds us of those things that Jesus has said to us (***John 14:26***). We must learn to depend on the indwelling Holy Spirit to show us how to discern what God is saying to us in His word. We want to be enlightened. We want to be inspired. We want God's word to help us get through the day. We want God's word to help us to be of help to others. These outline some of the things I ask for before I begin my time in the word. And I encourage you to do the same. Hands down God will show you His faithfulness regarding this!

While I am in Bible Immersion, I continue to pray—especially when I find myself not engaging my heart and my mind. When I find that I am daydreaming or taking on a "get 'er done" mindset, I have to stop and pray.

When I was first starting Bible Immersion I would sometimes get an overwhelming urge to not complete the assignment (especially when the particular part of the Bible was a difficult chapter or book to understand). If you are new at Bible Immersion, this urge to quit will come more often than not. Expect it. Ask God to take it away. You might pray in this manner: *{Dear Father, all of a sudden it feels hard again to do my Bible Immersion. I know that this is temptation, but I feel powerless to stop it. Please renew a willing Spirit in me to be a strong warrior for You. Let me not run away. Let me not grow weary. Let me stand firm in resisting this attack by Satan. In the name of Jesus I pray. Amen.}*

Prayer in the name of Jesus never fails! It keeps all of us going as long as we keep praying! And we can even ask for that if the struggle continues. Pray in this way:

{Dear Father, I have been sitting here struggling and I forgot that I don't need to struggle but to pray with fervency and belief. Empower me to do both of these things. You can do this! Give me the willingness and strength to pray until the temptation passes. In the name of Jesus I pray. Amen.}

3.

MY WEAPON AGAINST OVEREATING AND DEPRESSION

For the word of God is living and active, sharper than any two-edged sword, piercing to the division of soul and of spirit, of joints and of marrow, and discerning the thoughts and intentions of the heart. - Hebres

For as long as I can remember I had an ongoing struggle with overeating. It was how I came to the undeniable realization that I needed a Savior. A close second to my overeating was my battle with depression. The "voices" were the enemies and I knew them at a very early age. I could not defeat them. They would beat me to a pulp!

This is not the case today. First, God gave me rebirth through Jesus Christ. Then He taught me to hide Scripture in my heart. The Word is the powerful weapon of a true child of God. In Bible Immersion I have a deep encounter with the word each day. I read it. I listen to it. I write about it. I pray it.

When I was first looking for a solution to my struggle with these two foes, I was urged to look deep into my "baggage". I know today that the things that I focus upon can become bigger than life. I only have 24 hours in any given day. Instead of spending time dredging up the hurts and painful circumstances of the past, I choose to concentrate on my new identity in Christ.

I do not have to manufacture an inventory in order to face areas that need healing. When the time is right, in the course of going through the Bible again and again, God shows me these areas and at the same time equips me to take care of them.

*{Dear Father, You are showing me how to live. Your word is truly becoming a lamp to my feet and a light for my path (**Psalm 119:105**). Thank you for showing me how to soundly defeat overeating and depression. There is NOTHING Your word cannot do! I pray to keep immersing in Your word. I pray to keep encouraging others to do the same. In the name of Jesus I pray. Amen.}*

4.

GOD'S DAILY REMINDERS

The people of Judah have sinned again and again, and I will not let them go unpunished. They have rejected the instruction of the Lord, refusing to obey his decrees. They have been led astray by the same lies that deceived their ancestors.
~ Amos 2:4

God loves me and has given me many gifts. Problems arise when, in my flesh, the gifts become more important than the mission of God given to me. This was the difficulty that God addressed in the book of Amos.

The people of God were enjoying their riches to the hilt, while turning their backs on the poor and oppressed. They were called to be God's shepherds. Yet, they were trampling over the sheep in an effort to get more for themselves. So God sent his prophet Amos to warn them of the disaster that was coming, if they refused to repent.

God sends me daily wake-up calls in His word. These are the two important questions: 1) Will I take the time to read and study the word each day, and 2) Will I call on the Holy Spirit's power in order to live out what God is commanding? It is my choice, but I suffer greatly when I choose not to be in the word. Without the daily input of Scripture, my mind is drawn to the enticements of evil, and before long, the call of flesh becomes louder than the call of truth. And I wander off again!

{Dear Father, You have left us here to tell others that the curse has been broken! Help us to remember that our primary purpose is The Great Commission. The world must see Your resurrection power

demonstrated in our own lives. They must know that it is possible for them to have this power as well. Raise us up to resist the many temptations which threaten to lead us astray in this very day. Keep us out of denial and believing that we are too busy to stay immersed in Your word! In the name of Jesus we pray. Amen.}

5.

FEAR NOT

I have called you by name, you are mine. When you pass through the waters, I will be with you; and through the rivers, they shall not overwhelm you; when you walk through fire you shall not be burned, and the flame shall not consume you. For I am the LORD your God. ~ Isaiah 43:1-3

Scary times will come and go in this life—times when conditions are uncertain and circumstances are trying. But God has shown me that these are the times when I must pull in even closer to Him. The Lord almighty has shown me the power of hiding His word in my heart. As I immerse in the word of God I build highways for the Lord to enter into my situations.

In times past, I sat in darkness, closing off the light of Lord. I attempted to cover my fears by indulging in counterfeit pleasures. Other times I ran to "experts" believing that their answer would rid me of the anxieties of life. Sometimes I got relief. Unfortunately it was short-lived.

But God never forgot me. He reached into my world and showed me that what I needed could only be found in Him. Through Jesus Christ, God became real and up close. His love is making me fearless. I can suit up and show up for life. I can be of help to others. I can be part of the solution and not the problem. What a way to live!

{Dear Father, I pray to give You quality time in this day so that You can do your healing work in me. I pray to read Your word. I pray to study Your word. I pray to use Your word to direct every aspect of my life. Speak to my heart. Renew my mind. Fan up the gratitude

for my salvation and the passion to make You known. With all my heart, I pray to never forget this magnificent privilege of being Your child. My name is written in heaven. I have crossed over from death to life. I am eternally gratefully! In the name of Jesus I give thanks and praise. Amen.}

6.

REMEMBERING THE CALL UPON MY LIFE

And he said to them, "Go into all the world and proclaim the gospel to the whole creation. ~ Mark 16:15

Salvation has given me an eternal vision. I have been called to set my sights heavenward in Christ Jesus. There is work to be done for the Lord as I wait for His return. I must be careful not to let the devil trick me.

In this life I will come face to face with flesh. I will have to deal with people, places, and personalities that can make my work for the kingdom seem very hard. Circumstances can become difficult. I can start to feel overwhelmed. The devil in his craftiness can seize the opportunity to stir up my emotions. I can fight the wrong enemy and/or I give up in despair. I can forget that God's truth is greater than what I feel!

At these times I must remember what He has shown me in His word. I must purpose in my mind to focus on the goodness of God and not on the imperfections of life and mankind. The Lord blesses me each and every day as I labor side by side with Him. I have been given a purpose and a place. I have fellowship with Jesus and the joy of His constant presence. Why would I foolishly ignore these precious gifts by having my head turned in the wrong direction!

{Dear Father, open my eyes to the magnificence of my salvation! Though I was one who came to You late in life, You have not withheld any of the bounty that You lavish upon Your children. Thank you for Your favor. Thank you for giving me a new life that is eternally full and meaningful. In the name of Jesus I give thanks and pray. Amen.}

7.

DON'T FOOL YOURSELF!

The pride of your heart has deceived you, you who live in the clefts of the rock, in your lofty dwelling, who say in your heart, "Who will bring me down to the ground?" Though you soar aloft like the eagle, though your nest is set among the stars, from there I will bring you down, declares the Lord.
~ Obadiah 1:3-4

Edom was the home of the city of Petra. Petra was magnificently built in the clefts of the rocks. To the eyes of man, it seems that this city was impenetrable. But God wanted Edom to know that nothing was going to stand in the way of Him bringing judgment upon them. When the time was right, He warned them that He was surely going to bring them down!

In my flesh I can be in grand denial—thinking that I know too much to ever return to the devastation that once characterized my life...NOT!!!

Though I cannot be snatched out of the hand of God (***John 10:28-30***), I can sin and follow the dictates of my flesh. I can make my life very miserable by taking my eyes off of my Savior and living in the darkness.

Because God loves me and I belong to Him, He will correct me and reprimand my rebelliousness...and this can be quite ugly!

{Dear Father, help me to remember that love is a much better teacher than pain! Fill me up with the Holy Spirit so that I might have the willingness and strength to keep in step with the Spirit. In the name of Jesus I pray. Amen.}

8.

MY GREAT HIGH PRIEST

The priest shall make atonement for him before the LORD, and he shall be forgiven for any of the things that one may do and thereby become guilty. ~ Leviticus 6:7

Throughout the day, I have periods of "temporary amnesia". I forget who I am in Christ and I sin. I covet what another has. I contend with my sisters in the Lord. I murmur and complain about life. I think that I am still my flesh and I let evil control me.

If I had lived in the time of Moses, I would have had to go to the priest, and he would have had to make an offering for me before the Lord. If I was rich, I would have had to bring a bull or a lamb or a goat. If I was not rich, I would have had to bring a bird or fine flour. It would take quite some time to do these things I'm sure. And knowing "the world, the flesh, and the devil", I would have had many opportunities to change my mind about the matter and "stew" in my sin.

God in his mercy chose to give me life in this period of history. I have a Great High Priest and His name is Jesus Christ. He has already paid the price for my sin. I do not have to take anything to Him except my heart and tell Him of my sorrow for missing the mark again in living. He is faithful when I do this, and He purifies me from all unrighteousness.

{Dear Lord, Your grace is amazing to me. It speaks to me of Your great, great love for me. This love compels me to turn from my sin and live a life again that is pleasing to You. This love causes me to want to share with others, this same love that You pour into me. Thank you for being my great High Priest. May I sing of Your love forever!}

9.

SHOWING TRUE LOVE AND COMPASSION

Therefore be imitators of God, as beloved children. And walk in love, as Christ loved us and gave himself up for us, a fragrant offering and sacrifice to God. ~ Ephesians 5:1-2

Ham was the son of a spiritual giant. The Bible says that *"**Noah was a righteous man, blameless among the people of his time, and he walked with God (6:9)"***. Ham had witnessed his father's spiritual strength through many years of building an ark and surviving the punishing worldwide flood upon the earth.

But despite all of these things, Noah was human, and like us all, capable of forgetting our connection with God and falling into fleshly behavior. Noah got drunk and laid naked—exposing his body in his drunken state. (***Genesis 9:21***)

Ham used the opportunity to pass on some "juicy gossip" to his brothers about the incident (***Genesis 9:22***). But his brothers did not take the bait: ***Shem and Japheth took a garment and laid it across their shoulders; then they walked in backward and covered their father's naked body. Their faces were turned the other way so that they would not see their father naked. (Genesis 9:23)***

{Dear Father, the temptation to try to build myself up at the expense of another is always available. Please keep me strong to side-step the temptation. I pray to remember that regardless of how disappointed I feel about the behavior of another, You have called me to pray for them and not to criticize them. Keep me prayerful today. Keep me in Your word so that I do not conform to behavior that is common place in the world around me. I pray these things in the name of Jesus. Amen.}

10.

SEEKING GOD FIRST

And rising very early in the morning, while it was still dark, he departed and went out to a desolate place, and there he prayed. ~ Mark 2:35

In my morning quiet time I can refuel my thinking and remember that I have been reborn! Moreover, when I give the Lord the firstfruits of the daily hours of my life, He gives back my time with overflowing abundance.

Jesus knew the importance of solitude. I am learning to follow His lead. At the start of the day I seek spaces and places where I can ponder deeply the goodness of God, and give thanks for His love for me. My recovery requires quality time alone with God. In these times I can pour out my heart to Him fearlessly and listen for His response. Even when I encounter "interruptions", I have learned to continue to make the effort to seek out these times and God has blessed my obedience.

{Dear Father, thank you for another day of having the opportunity to learn from Your word. I pray for the willingness and strength to have some quality time with You at the start of each day. Cause my heart to touch Your heart. Fill me with the remembrance that I am dearly loved and highly favored by You. You are my "Abba Father". I pray to not let the world's enticements or the devil's lies keep me from this special time with You. I pray in the name of Jesus. Amen.}

11.

THERE'S NOTHING MY GOD CANNOT DO!

And he awoke and rebuked the wind and said to the sea, "Peace! Be still!" And the wind ceased, and there was a great calm. He said to them, "Why are you so afraid? Have you still no faith?" 41 And they were filled with great fear and said to one another, "Who then is this, that even the wind and the sea obey him?"~ Mark 4:39-41

My finite mind would like to place the power of God in a box. According to my human thinking there are things in my life that concern God, and there are things that I need not bother taking to Him. I am learning not to limit the scope of God's concern. If something is big enough to show up on my radar screen of anxiety, then it is big enough to "take it to the Lord in prayer." My motto has become **Philippians 4:6 (the NLT version) ~ *Don't worry about anything; instead, pray about everything. Tell God what you need, and thank him for all he has done.***

{Dear Father, thank you for teaching me not to censor my prayers. You can take the honest confessions of my thoughts and feelings. There is NOTHING that I cannot pray about. You love me. You listen to me. You show me time and time again how much You care for me. Thank you so, so much, Lord, for showing me this way to live. I want to stay deep in Your word today because I don't want anything hindering my ability to hear You. I don't want to miss the next miracle You have in store for me. I pray and give thanks in the name of Jesus Christ. Amen.}

12.

WHEN SHEEP REBEL

Now there was no water for the congregation. And they assembled themselves together against Moses and against Aaron. And the people quarreled with Moses and said, "Would that we had perished when our brothers perished before the Lord! Why have you brought the assembly of the Lord into this wilderness, that we should die here, both we and our cattle?~ Numbers 20:2-4

As Christians we are called to lead and nurture the flock of God. We are His leaders. Nevertheless a call to shepherd is not a guarantee that the sheep will willingly follow. Moses and Aaron certainly knew this!

Leadership is not for the weak! It's erroneous to believe that a call from the Lord will not be marked by setbacks and challenges. Testing through difficult situations, and by way of difficult people is a given. Nevertheless, as leaders, we cannot react in our flesh when conditions get hard and people rebel. If we forget, we can be led into sin and will have to suffer the consequences of our own disobedience. Moses found this out. He lost the privilege of entering the promise land with his people because of this.

{Dear Father, please do not let me be taken aback when people lash out in anger and bitterness. I pray to remember that EVERYBODY has flesh and every one of us has misbehaved in hurtful ways. In the midst of difficult encounters, please keep me coming to You so that I might continue to respond in wisdom, in truth, and in love. In the name of Jesus I pray. Amen.}

13.

READ. STUDY. APPLY.

"And when he sits on the throne of his kingdom, he shall write for himself in a book a copy of this law, approved by the Levitical priests. And it shall be with him, and he shall read in it all the days of his life, that he may learn to fear the Lord his God by keeping all the words of this law and these statutes, and doing them, that his heart may not be lifted up above his brothers, and that he may not turn aside from the commandment, either to the right hand or to the left, so that he may continue long in his kingdom, he and his children, in Israel."~ Deuteronomy 17:18-19

Before entering the Promise Land, Moses gave the people guidelines for any future king they might have. Included in these was a directive that the king must write down a copy of the Lord's statutes, keep this copy with him, and read these statutes daily as long as he lived. The purpose of doing this, Moses told the people, was to teach obedience and fear of the Lord. Additionally, this immersion would serve to prevent him from pride and walking away from the tremendous promise of blessings that the Lord had reserved for him and his descendants.

Because I belong to Jesus, I have been given the promise of tremendous blessings, too. If I do not know God's way or remember God's way, I will go back into my "default" way of acting, speaking, and thinking in my flesh. Bible immersion cannot be a once and a while thing with me. God has shown me that I am in a war zone and my enemy is vicious and smart. Why would I want to jeopardize this wonderful life of deep and true abundance? Why would I deny my children (and my children's children) the opportunity of experiencing a richer life?

*{Dear Father, You have opened my eyes to the busyness of the evil one. He is proclaiming his agenda and way of life on screens, in books, on radio, on billboards, in the mouths of others...You name it, he has his finger in the pot! Please, Lord, keep me diligent "not to conform to the pattern of this world, but to be transformed by the renewing of my mind" (**Romans 12:2**). Keep me purging my thinking of any rebellious thoughts. I pray to practice humility, to stay abstinent, and to prayerfully live out Your word today. I pray in the name of Jesus. Amen.}*

14.

UNBELIEF

But now, since you didn't believe what I said, you will be silent and unable to speak until the child is born. For my words will certainly be fulfilled at the proper time. ~ Luke 1:20

Zechariah the priest was serving the Lord in the temple when an angel appeared to him in the sanctuary. The message that the angel was bringing was very, very good. Zechariah's prayers for his barren wife were going to be fulfilled and they would soon have a son!

At a time when Zechariah should have been jumping for joy, he was skeptical of the words of God that had been delivered to him. His punishment for his disbelief was that he would be unable to speak until his son was born. God's miracles in a life are limited only by lack of belief.

{Dear Father, please fill me with Your word so that I can sense the presence of untruth in my thinking. Teach me the language of the redeemed that will demolish all strongholds of unbelief. Please keep me vigilant to not let the devil use my mouth to sin. Keep speaking the truth and encouraging others to do the same. Help us all to live courageously today— not knocked to the sidelines by habitual sin, nor bowled over by fear. It's in the mighty name of Jesus that I pray. Amen.}

15.

DEEPER WATERS

"Put out into deep water, and let down the nets for a catch." Simon answered, "Master, we've worked hard all night and haven't caught anything. But because you say so, I will let down the nets." ~ Luke 5:4,5

As Jesus preached on the shores of Lake Gennesaret, many people pressed in to hear Him. Seeing two empty boats, Jesus got into the one that was owned by Simon Peter, and asked him to push it out into the lake, to better teach the crowd.

When Jesus had finished speaking to the people, He told Peter to go out into the deep part of the lake so that he would catch many fish. Simon was reluctant to do this since he had fished all night and had not caught a thing. Nevertheless, he obeyed what Jesus told him to do and was greatly blessed by his obedience. He caught so many fish, that he had to call the other boat for help and the fish that they pulled in filled both boats to the point of sinking!

*{Dear Father, forgive me when I fear going out into deeper waters because of past failures. I pray to remember that You are the author of all that is truly good in my life. Give me courage to walk out in faith upon your promises and revealed truth. I pray not to be haunted by my past, but to trust in You for a magnificent future. Keep me out of habitual sin. Keep me clear in my thinking. Keep me deep in Your word and knowing right from wrong. In You I am able to do immeasurably more that all I ask or imagine **(Ephesians 3:20)**. Thank you for loving me so much! In Jesus' name I pray. Amen.}*

16.

MY BIBLE IMMERSION STORY

For the word of God is alive and active. Sharper than any double-edged sword, it penetrates even to dividing soul and spirit, joints and marrow; it judges the thoughts and attitudes of the heart. ~ Hebrews 4:12

Fourteen years prior to surrendering to Jesus Christ, I was heavily involved in secular recovery for overeating. Around year ten I became willing to diligently follow the food guidelines that were told to me. I got order with my food, and I lost the 70 pounds I needed. I was told that I would not be able to maintain my abstinence if I did not continue to go to meetings and work the steps.

Since I had known the devastation of relapse and bingeing, I had the willingness to work hard to prevent this from happening again. Nevertheless, despite my thorough step work and my squeaky clean food, the darkness in my soul still remained. I began fearing that I would lose my abstinence by self-sabotage.

God in His mercy brought me to Christian Radio. On Christian Radio I heard the gospel of Jesus Christ as it had never been taught in my liberal church. I surrendered my life to Jesus and became "Born Again". Shortly after this I was inspired to read through the Bible each year.

As I read and studied the word, it did not take long for me to realize that abstinence was part of God's plan for my life. By this time I had worked through the 12 steps countless times. After just one year of reading through the Bible I knew "hands down" that I was getting a better return on writing about scripture and praying with scripture than any manmade solution for staying out of the food. This process of reading scripture, thinking about scripture, and praying scripture gave birth to Bible Immersion. This process was (and still is) unsurpassed by all that I have ever tried for food recovery!

As I dug deeper into the word, I saw how sinful my compulsive eating had been. Today I know that the devil uses compulsive eating, depression, addictions, procrastination, wasting money and time, (you fill in the blank) to keep a Christian diverted and "running in place." I am convinced that these maladies can be blown out of the water when Jesus is pursued through sincere, consistent deep time in the word of God.

I refuse today to knowingly be used by Satan. I don't just teach Bible Immersion, I live it! Meeting Jesus intimately each day is a priority. I want to be all that God died to make me. I pray to live all my days being fueled and equipped by Scripture and teaching others to do the same.

{Dear Father, I pray to always stay immersed in Your word. Please keep me sitting at the feet of Jesus and drinking from the fount of living water. Keep me encouraging others to walk in this marvelous way. Please keep me abstinent so that my thinking is clear and I am not just merely "talking the talk". I pray in the holy name of Jesus. Amen.}

17.

STANDING FIRM THROUGH HARD TIMES

Finally, be strong in the Lord and in his great power. Put on the full armor of God so that you can fight against the devil's evil tricks. ~ Ephesians 6:10

I was very surprised to learn that times of suffering could actually increase because I had made the decision to follow Jesus. Today it makes perfect sense. Before, I was no real threat to the kingdom of darkness. Once I made the decision to turn away from being used by evil, and began walking in the footsteps of Jesus, my progress became the devil's defeat! Seasons of suffering will weave in and out of my life until Jesus comes for me (***John 16:33***). It takes maturity and determination to keep an attitude of joy in hard times.

It is easy to forget that this world is not my home. I am on a journey. God has saved me through the blood of Jesus and He wants me to take this Good News out to others who do not know Him yet, or who have forgotten about Him.

I have an enemy. It is not another human being, but it is the devil himself. He tries many ways to discourage me on this journey. He would love to get me back into compulsive overeating because he knows my history of eating addiction. Since this is not an option today, he tries to discourage me with negativity.

Thank the Lord that I know today that as I stay away from known sinful behaviors and stay in God's word, I will be empowered to rise above any and all emotional turmoil. The battle and suffering might seem endless, but they are temporary (***2 Corinthians 4:18***)! With

God's help, I will continue to resist the devil and he will flee. I know, because God has told me so in His Word! (***James 4:7***)

*{Dear Father, thank you for teaching me that my present suffering does not compare to the joy I am going to experience when Your glory is revealed (**1 Peter 4:12-13**). Nothing escapes You. You are all-knowing and You love me dearly. Keep me abstinent—No Matter What! Strengthen me to stand firm and to wait expectantly for the joy that You will reveal in this day. I pray in the name of Jesus. Amen.}*

18.

THE WAY, THE TRUTH, THE LIFE

Dear friends, do not believe every spirit, but test the spirits to see whether they are from God, because many false prophets have gone out into the world. This is how you can recognize the Spirit of God: Every spirit that acknowledges that Jesus Christ has come in the flesh is from God. ~ 1 John 4:1-2

There was a time in my life when I had no idea how to handle intense and sudden feelings, so I drowned them in food. Overtime, I found secular fellowships where I could speak out honestly about my feelings to others. These groups were committed to practicing confidentiality and not judging one another. I felt safe and accepted. Instead of eating over my feelings I could share them, and this brought me much relief from feeling so isolated and lonely. Moreover, as others shared about their problems and solutions, I began to use their methods in my own life. I thought for quite some time that this was the answer to all my problems—one person helping another.

God wants me to be in fellowship with others. God wants me to help others. But if Jesus is not genuinely at the center it is dangerous. The Bible reminds me in **Psalm 127:1 ~ Unless the Lord builds the house, the builders labor in vain.** Twice in **Proverbs (16:25 and 14:12)** there is the warning: **There is a way that seems right to a man, but in the end it leads to death.**

*{Dear Father, there are many places of learning, but only one source of truth. Your Son Jesus is the way, the truth, and the life (**John 14:6**). Thank you for teaching me that healing is more important than relief and only Jesus heals. Keep me wise and discerning regarding the friends and the fellowships I embrace. Keep me pointing others to Jesus. In His holy name I pray. Amen.}*

19.

WORKERS OF EVIL

Depart from me, all you workers of evil, for the LORD has heard the sound of my weeping. ~ Psalm 6:8

Long before I knew what they were, I had dealings with "the voices." According to the voices, I could do nothing right. There was always an ongoing negative commentary from them streaming through my life. If I accomplished much, they were quick to point out the one thing I had left undone. If I had helped many, they would remind me of an offense that I had made (real or imagined). It is little wonder, now as I look back, that I always felt at the bottom of the heap.

God in His mercy taught me the true story of salvation. He taught me that every human being comes into the world with an innate tendency to make wrong choices. The Bible calls it a "sin nature". In order to offset this sin nature, I needed God to come into my heart in the form of the Holy Spirit. I received this Holy Spirit when: 1) I confessed my sinfulness, 2) understood that Jesus, God the Son, died a sacrificial death to pay the penalty for me, and 3) surrendered my life to Jesus to be my Savior and my Lord forever.

I belong to Jesus. He is my protector. His Spirit lives within me and nothing can stand against me. When the voices start, I am learning to turn my face to the Lord and stand firm through the power of His word, and they flee!

{Dear Father, for so many years the voices crushed every ounce of self-esteem that I could muster. I thank you, because this is not true

today. I can live my life fearlessly today because I have a Savior. I don't have to run from life. I don't have to run to food or ANY false god today. You are my shield and my protector. I give thanks with praise in the name of Jesus Christ. Amen.}

20.

BUILD EACH OTHER UP

If your brother sins against you, go and show him his fault, just between the two of you. If he listens to you, you have won your brother over. ~ Matthew 18:15

The devil works hard to tear apart the Christian community. While I am "scratching out the eyes" of my sister or brother in Christ, the devil is sitting back in ease while his work is being done for him.

Every human being who has made a sincere confession of faith in the finished work of Jesus Christ is my brother and sister in the Lord. My tie to them is stronger than biological ties because we are bound together forever by the blood of Jesus Christ. We are one body. We share the same Spirit.

Each one of us in the body has the capability of forgetting that we have been redeemed. We all can be in our flesh and flesh on anyone is ugly! Our responsibility when we observe a sister or brother in their flesh is to pray that they will come to their senses and escape the devil's trap (see **2 Timothy 2: 24 – 26**). Furthermore, we can ask to be set free from bitterness toward them. We can pray to be filled with a spirit of reconciliation and forgiveness.

{Dear Father, thank you for New Life in the Spirit. Help me to watch and pray so that the devil cannot use me to hurt and destroy my brothers and sisters in Christ. Fill me with the love of Jesus so that I am a vital part of building Your church and not tearing it down. I pray to encourage my "siblings" to do the same. In the name of Jesus Christ I pray. Amen.}

21.

KEEPING THE MAIN THING THE MAIN THING

"Of all the commandments, which is the most important?" "The most important one," answered Jesus, "is this: 'Hear, O Israel, the Lord our God, the Lord is one. Love the Lord your God with all your heart and with all your soul and with all your mind and with all your strength.~ Mark 12:28, 29

I have been given the greatest gift in all the world. I have been saved! I have the Holy Spirit living in me. My future has been secured. I am going to live forever with my Lord in heaven. No one or nothing can ever separate me from my glorious destiny.

When I think deeply about this magnificent gift and keep God's truth before me, I am able to move forward through the circumstances of this life with rock solid certainty. When I lose focus, I flounder and worry and become a poor witness for the Lord.

Herein lies the key: I must keep the love of God ever before me--in all that I think, say, and do.

{Dear Father, please forgive me for the many times when I have worried and fretted about things in this life. Help me to mature as a Christian and to trust You more. Grow me up so that I can make You proud for choosing me to be Your child. I am so very grateful for my salvation! I pray and give thanks in the name of Jesus Christ. Amen.}

22.

DIVERSION

That they will come to their senses and escape from the trap of the devil, who has taken them captive to do his will. ~ 2 Timothy 2:26

Because I belong to Jesus Christ, I am now an enemy of the devil. He will do all he can to slow me down and to take me out. He knows that the time is short regarding the things that must be done for God's kingdom. I am convinced that one of his most used tools is diversion.

With diversion, the devil can attack without really seeming like he is attacking. This is why the eating disorder is so dangerous. He can get Christians spending tons of time "majoring in the minors". If you think I am kidding, the next time you are in a conversation with other Christians, see how much time is spent talking about food (eating, weight, exercise, body image, appearance, etc.) as opposed to talking about Spiritual growth and development.

Truly, I am not talking about a stoic lifestyle, but I am making an appeal to "do the math". We all have 24 hours in a day. We have been given the greatest gift—the gift of eternal life in Jesus Christ! We have been given the charge to make Him known to a world that is searching desperately for the answer. He is the answer!

{Dear Father, thank you for showing me just how much time has been freed up by just getting my food in order. Thank you for my abstinence. You have given me a sanity and peace about food and eating that I would have never thought possible. Please keep me deep in Your word so that I am giving a clear and truthful message to all. I pray in the name of Jesus. Amen.}

23.

MARCHING ORDERS

The Spirit of the LORD is upon me, for he has anointed me to bring Good News to the poor. He has sent me to proclaim that captives will be released, that the blind will see, that the oppressed will be set free. ~ Luke 14:18

God is an intelligent designer. He has a plan and a purpose for each person that He creates. Even when what He does seems random, God know what He wants.

God saved me by the blood of Jesus. I am so very, very grateful for this salvation. I have been called to take the message of salvation to those who do not know Jesus yet. I do this by both word and deed. Those who observe my life should know that God indwells me and that I belong to Him.

I have also been called to remind those who know Jesus to wake up and realize that our days are numbered and our time is short. We can no longer justify wasting this precious God-given gift of time. In the power of the Spirit we can resolve to stop aiding the devil by losing sight of the true "primary purpose", the Great Commission (***Matthew 28:18-20***).

{Dear Father, You have given me my marching orders. I am to know You well so that I can effectively make You known. Please keep me out of the food. Please keep into Your word—drinking it in and living it out, each and every day. I pray to turn away from all thoughts, actions, and attitudes that compete with keeping You first place in my life. I pray in the name of Jesus. Amen.}

24.

MY HELP COMES FROM THE LORD

***Our eyes look to the LORD our God, till he
has mercy upon us. ~ Psalm 123:2***

One of the first things that I am called to remember in the book of James is that I will have trials as I grow in my spiritual life. The mature way to experience these trials (see ***James 1:2, 3***) is with an attitude of joy. This is just the opposite of what the flesh tells me. The flesh urges me to verbalize again and again how badly I am presently feeling. The devil, who controls the flesh, knows that if I continue to vent in this manner, I will eventually start feeling some unfairness on God's part. I pout. I start feeling bitter and in the past, this was the perfect backdrop for a binge.

Regardless of what "the voices" say, God is all-loving and God is all-merciful to me. Nothing occurs in my life that He doesn't know about. If I have cried out to God for relief, and if I have solicited prayers from other believers for my concerns, then it's time to practice obedience while I wait for the change. There is kingdom work before me that is calling my name. I pray to fan up the Spirit's power, to "lift my eyes to the hills", and to walk faithfully ahead into this day.

{Dear Father, keep me in Your word today. Keep Your word in me so that I can know Your Truth. Thank you for reminding me that despite my feelings, I have much to be joyful about. I am saved. I am abstinent. I am loved by my creator and Lord. Thank you for keeping me. Thank you for being my shade in the scorching times of life—now and forevermore. I am Your servant and I pray to serve You well today and with gladness. I pray in the name of Jesus. Amen.}

25.

RISING ABOVE THE FLESH

Do not be overcome by evil, but overcome evil with good. ~ Romans 12:21

Through Jesus Christ I experience the favor of God. This is why it is so very important that I immerse myself in the Bible. In the Word of God I grow in my knowledge and love of Jesus. I have been saved by His blood. My life is now protected against eternal destruction. As I stay grounded in Jesus, other people benefit. Even when others choose to act in their flesh, I don't have to react in mine. Through the lessons from Jesus' life and the power of His indwelling Spirit, I am able to respond to others in love. Instead of "repaying" evil with evil, I can overcome evil with good.

{Dear Father, I pray to remember that You have called me to a life of supernatural love. Help me to remember that we all have flesh. Help me to remember that I have the Holy Spirit's power to rise above flesh. Keep me determined to live a joyful, giving and forgiving life. Keep me faithful in prayer and living harmoniously with others. Thank you for the blessing of this new life in Christ. I pray that in all I do others will sense the fervor and zeal that You have infused in me for You. I pray in the name of Jesus. Amen.}

26.

STANDING FIRM

Therefore, my dear brothers, stand firm. Let nothing move you. Always give yourselves fully to the work of the Lord, because you know that your labor in the Lord is not in vain. ~ 1 Corinthians 15:58

I have to keep in mind that every period of good progress in my life will be followed by a counter-offensive by the devil. At times he seems to bring out a huge battalion. Things feel extremely hard and my flesh starts crying for a place to "sit down for a while."

I thank God that His voice of truth is louder than the voice of the enemy. God reminds me that I am not alone. He is with me and because of His great power I can stand strong and keep my position. Backsliding is not a requirement.

{Dear Father, please continue to strengthen me in this war zone called life. Please give me the willingness and the strength to spend quality time in Your word today. I pray to walk out boldly in the promises that You have made on my life. I pray in the name of Jesus. Amen.}

27.

TRUE INSPIRATION

You will know the truth, and the truth will set you free.
~ John 8:32

In the world today there are so many voices. Some are helpful. Some are harmful. Some build us up. Some tear us down. As children of God, we are called to know God's word and to speak His language.

When we speak the language of the redeemed, we become true encouragers. We can have confidence that our words will not tether people to another crutch, but will empower them to soar. Our words will not cause them to give up, but will help them to stand firm.

Only God is capable of giving such inspiration and this is what Bible immersion is all about. We are called to know the word and to use the word in our own lives. We are called to share the word with others so that they will be encouraged. (See **Isaiah 50:4**.)

{Dear Father, keep us deep in Your word each day. Keep Your word deep in us. Keep us away from our known areas of sinful enticements. We want to know the truth. We want to remember Your anointing and the call that You have on our lives. You have set us free for freedom and we are eternally grateful! We pray and give thanks in the name of Jesus. Amen.}

28.

SPEAK LIFE

He must hold firmly to the trustworthy message as it has been taught, so that he can encourage others by sound doctrine. ~ Titus 1:9

My mouth can bring hope to another or can be used to discourage and destroy ambition. God calls me to stay in His word so that the words I speak line up with the truth of the Bible. Because I am surrounded by a world that does not know Jesus, I could easily be speaking the enemy's language that has been dressed up as light. I did this for many years. I never want to do this again! The Lord is the source of light. I pray that each day I give Him time to teach me and train me, to enrich and inspire me so that when I speak, I speak life.

{Dear Father, keep me having the willingness and the strength to immerse myself in Your word each day. As you feed me with true food, you call me to turn to others and share with them Your empowering word. In giving truth to others, I sense Your presence even more and my blessings multiply! Thank you for loving me so dearly. I pray and give thanks in the name of Jesus. Amen.}

29.

UNGODLY COUNSEL

Blessed is the man who walks not in the counsel of the wicked, nor stands in the way of sinners, nor sits in the seat of scoffers. ~ Psalm 1:1

When I was a young adult I spent "gobs" of time poring over fashion magazines. I was seeking a way to be skinny, while at the same time have the freedom to eat whatever I wished. I believed that the people that I saw on the pages of these publications held the key to my ultimate success to reach this goal.

I studied their advice—hanging on to their every word as the gospel truth. To the best of my ability I emulated their lifestyle. They were like deity to me. Needless to say, my morals ran aground as I caught more from those pages than just merely advice about weight control and fashion.

{Dear Father, You are teaching me that my mind is a powerful thing. I pray to stay alert—quick to dispel any thought that is not Godly and moving me toward a stronger life in Christ Jesus. The internet, magazines, newspapers and TV can affect me more than I can ever believe! I pray to guard my ears and my eyes at all times. I pray for those who are struggling with the food. I pray that they will honestly look at the amount of time that they spend under the counsel of the world as opposed to Your counsel in the Word. Please change their heart and open their eyes. Please continue to do the same for me. I pray this in the name of Jesus Christ. Amen.}

30.

THE BEST WAY

"Enter through the narrow gate; for the gate is wide and the way is broad that leads to destruction, and there are many who enter through it. For the gate is small and the way is narrow that leads to life, and there are few who find it. ~ Matthew 7:13-14

On most days, what I feel in my life is a flooding by the peace of God. But there are days when I feel the loneliness of marching to a different drum. New friends seem taken aback that I don't just eat whatever or whenever I want. Others are curious about my passion for Bible immersion, but only as long as it does not interfere with their thinking that they are exempt!

God is showing me that there is no greater life than pursuing Jesus and finding one's delight in Him. I have been called to teach this through both word and deed. God will keep me standing firm in this call even when it is not easy. He wants the world to know that Jesus alone is "the Way, the Truth, and the Life" (***John 14:6***).

{Dear Father, may I never forget how lost and confused I was before I found Jesus. May I never stop caring for those who will perish if I fail to live Jesus out before them. Keep the narrow way before me. Keep me out of the food and immersed in Your word so that I keep maturing in my faith. Fill me up with Your Holy Spirit so that I am not led astray by what I feel. Thank you, Jesus, for You never leave me or forsake me. I am yours forever and the knowledge of this fills me with great joy! I pray and give thanks in your holy name. Amen.}

31.

MOST IMPORTANT

He said, "Do not lay your hand on the boy or do anything to him, for now I know that you fear God, seeing you have not withheld your son, your only son, from me." ~ Genesis 22:12

God did a most remarkable thing for Abraham and Sarah. He kept His promise to them and brought them a son—even though biologically it seemed impossible (***Genesis 21:1-3***). Nevertheless, God made it clear to Abraham that any gift that He gives must never be more important than He is. God tested Abraham (***Genesis 22***) to see if He understood this important principle. Abraham passed the test!

When I sincerely surrender my most precious possessions to God, at that very moment I am demonstrating fear of the Lord. At that very moment I am saying to God, and to the world that He is most important! PERIOD!

Many times I feel that I am mature in my surrender to the Lord, but God shows me that I am still very much a work in progress. Nevertheless, when I practice "letting go" with a loving and peaceful attitude, I sense a victory in this area and I am encouraged that God himself will help me to learn to fear Him more and more.

For God is working in you, giving you the desire and the power to do what pleases him. ~ Philippians 2:13

{Dear Father, thank you for another day mature in faith. Please continue to grow me up. I hold on too tightly to what You provide and in doing so, I forget about You. When I pray, help me to let go of whatever I am doing so that I can be surrendered heart to heart to

You. Thank you for the many lessons of faith that You show to me in Your word. Thank you for the "great cloud of witnesses" that spur me on by their examples of surrender. I am so grateful that I am not alone. I give thanks and pray in the name of Jesus. Amen.}

32.

GOD'S WONDERFUL TRUTH

Open my eyes to see the wonderful truths in your instructions. I am only a foreigner in the land. ~ Psalm 119:18, 19

This world is not my final destination. Jesus has gone before me to prepare a wonderful place with Him in heaven (***John 14:1-3***). I have been left here for a while because I am needed to bring God's light into dark places. I have been called to live my life as Jesus lived His life—filled with the power of the Spirit, proclaiming the freeing Good News, and reminding everyone that He is coming back!

The word of God shows me how to do this important work. I don't have to pull back in fear of inadequacy. The Lord is with me, He is equipping me, and He is filling me with His peace.

{Dear Father, what a delightful way to live. Despite the ups and downs of life, You have shown me how to stay joyful and full of Your peace. You have given me a purpose and a place. You are teaching me to know Your word and to live it out in the Spirit. This is the true, abundant life! Thank you for saving me and entrusting me to take this Good News out into the world today. Please keep me immersed in Your word. I pray in the name of Jesus. Amen.}

33.

FAVORITISM

If you show favoritism, you sin. ~ James 2:9

Of all of Jacob's sons, everyone knew that Joseph was his favorite. When Jacob thought that his brother Esau was coming to kill him and his family, he gave Joseph and his mother the most protected place (***Genesis 33:1-2***). In later days, Jacob even made Joseph a special coat of many colors and gave it to him. This unfortunate thoughtlessness caused great jealousy and hatred to grow in his other sons toward Joseph (***Genesis 37:2-4***).

{Dear Father, thank you for another day of learning from Your word. I pray to delight in all my children with equanimity! Convict me of my sin in this area. Please give me the willingness and the strength to amend my wrongs. May I keep Jesus before me as my divine model for life. Help me to see all people through His holy eyes of love. I pray in the name of Jesus Christ. Amen.}

34.

KEEPING THE LORD THE HIGHEST PRIORITY

You are my God; I shall seek You earnestly; My soul thirsts for You, my flesh yearns for You, In a dry and weary land where there is no water. ~ Psalm 63:1

In every hour of my day, in every minute of each hour, I have an opportunity to get off track in my thinking. I have a better chance of staying on track and getting back on track when I lose my way, when I give God the "first-fruits" of my day. For me this means starting my day with some heart to heart time with the Lord. As a woman who has emotional eating and food obsession in her history, quiet time is not optional—"it is a required course"!

With many years now of practicing the spiritual discipline of a morning quiet time, it is not a hardship to do, but a joy! I have seen both sides of the coin and I like living this way so much better! I like not having to struggle with the food. I like not having the extremes of high anxiety and deep depression that used to characterize my life. I like not having such a low self-esteem that I had to kill myself trying to prove that I WAS good enough.

I experience the presence of the Lord as I prayerfully immerse myself in His word each morning. He reminds me that I am greatly loved and highly favored. He floods me with a peace that the world does not understand, yet can never take away.

{Dear Father, thank you for teaching me that the willingness to be disciplined is a gift and not a hardship. May I keep Jesus before me in all that I do. May I seek to know Him and love Him better each day. May others come to be drawn to Jesus by sensing His presence in my life. In the name of Jesus I give thanks and pray. Amen.}

35.

WALK AWAY FROM THE TUBE

***Be on your guard against the yeast of the
Pharisees and Sadducees. ~ Matthew 16:11***

I am told that in my neighborhood we were one of the first ones to have TV in our home. This was in the early 50's and programming was scarce. With no all-night TV and only one station, TV did not affect my early childhood that much.

But as an adolescent, programming expanded and later with the introduction of cable, I became a full-fledged TV junkie! I did not know then what I know now, that my thinking was being reprogrammed and my appetite was being stimulated in ways that ran counter to the Godly values that my family upheld.

TV affected the way I talked, the way I dressed, the things I day-dreamed about, and definitely the way I ate! Food that I was not even THINKING about became something that I had to have! TV also affected my activity level. I no longer had time to ride my bicycle and roller skate with my friends because I had to see the next episode of whatever.

When I became serious about abstinence, my interaction with TV was one of the first things that had to dramatically change. Today I make it a point to be very, very careful about what I watch and how much I take in—both on the TV and on the internet.

{Dear Father, thank you for another day of abstinence and learning from Your word. You are showing me that the devil is busy and his tactics are sneaky. Help me to remember that I cannot mindlessly

take in evil and think that I will be unaffected. Please fill me with Your truth so that I can keep a guard against those "delightful" things that poison my heart and steal my time. When I am tempted, please give me the willingness and strength, to pray for willingness and strength! It's in the name of the Lord Jesus Christ that I pray. Amen.}

36.

RELAPSE—BIBLE STYLE

And the people of Israel again did what was evil in the sight of the LORD. ~ Judges 13:1

Despite all that the Lord did for the Israelites, they continued to have periods of walking away from Him. As punishment, the Lord would withdraw His protection over the nation and the people would experience severe oppression from their enemies.

When the suffering became overwhelming, the people would cry out to the Lord and He would send a leader, called a judge. For the most part, these judges were men who could help to bring about military victory against the enemy and thus stop the oppression.

When the oppression would stop, the people would experience a period of prosperity and gratitude for their deliverance. Unfortunately, it wasn't long before the people got so caught up in their good that they forgot about their God...and the cycle would begin again.

{Dear Father, I pray that I have learned my lesson for the rest of my life. Your love can never be forgotten. Neither can it be taken for granted. You are love and the greatness of this love can never take second place to anything! I pray to dig deeply into Your word today so that I can know You better and to love You more. I pray to turn away from all my idols, especially the grand idol of my past—overeating. Your love has transformed me. I trust in your love. I rejoice in your love. In the name of Jesus I give thanks and praise. Amen.}

37.

LIGHT TO ALL

"You are the light of the world. A city set on a hill cannot be hidden; nor does anyone light a lamp and put it under a basket, but on the lamp stand, and it gives light to all who are in the house. ~ Matthew 5:14-15

God has a path marked out for my feet each day. The devil, my adversary, will do all he can to divert me from this way. He loves to get me involved in "cat fights" where I am scratching out the eyes of others and wasting time pointing out the shortcomings of their flesh.

Every human being on this planet can lose their way and let the flesh take control. At all times, God wants me to have a loving and forgiving heart. As human beings we need encouraging examples of Spirit-controlled living. We don't need harsh criticism and thoughtless put-downs. God has placed Christians in the world to be light bringers. I pray that God can use me to be a light on the hill today.

{Dear Father, thank you for showing me how compulsive overeating was destroying my life. Thank you for showing me how delightful it is to have deep fellowship with You through Bible immersion. I pray to remember that You have kingdom work for me to do each and every day. Nothing is more important than living my life in a way that points others to Jesus. Please show me the areas in my life where I allow my flesh to be in control. I pray for the willingness and the strength to turn away from these dark places. It's in the name of Jesus that I pray. Amen.}

38.

GOOD WORK. GOD'S WORK.

For we are God's handiwork, created in Christ Jesus to do good works, which God prepared in advance for us to do. ~ Ephesians 2:10

In the Garden of Eden, even before the fall, God gave Adam the gift of meaningful work (**Genesis 2:15**). As a reborn child of God, it is a privilege and a joy to be productive. Good work is a means of carrying the message of the Good News of salvation. Productivity is a gift from the Lord.

Nevertheless, there are days when I start off and the voices seem to be having a heyday. On these days, my flesh is holding a megaphone and spouting off a never-ending stream of negativity about the "yuckiness" of everything! On these days I have to cry out to the Lord for strength to rise above the voices. In His mercy He reminds me to set my face like a flint (**Isaiah 50:7**), to fill up with Truth (**Psalm 119:10-12**), and to remember that I am not alone (**1 Peter 5:8-9**)! At the beginning of one of these battles, I feel the strain of having to push past my flesh. But praise the Lord—flesh is no match against Jesus Christ! (**James 4:7**)

{Dear Father, please keep me focused on Jesus and moving beyond my flesh. Open my eyes to the good work that You have planned for me to do today. Thank you for all that You are teaching me about life and living through Your word, the Bible. Please keep me abstinent and living in the freedom to fuel my body without slowing it down. I give thanks and praise in the name of Jesus Christ. Amen.}

39.

SOLOMON'S DOWNFALL

He had seven hundred wives of royal birth and three hundred concubines, and his wives led him astray. As Solomon grew old, his wives turned his heart after other gods. ~ 1 Kings 11:3-4

Even though Solomon was the child of an "illicit" union, he was beloved and favored by God (***2 Samuel 12:24***). Of all the sons of David, Solomon was the one that the Lord chose to sit on the throne after his father.

At the beginning of his time as king, Solomon walked with God. He showed his love for the Lord through obedience to the instructions given by his father (***1 Kings 3:3***), and in the same manner he prayed and gave sacrifices to the Lord (***1 Kings 8:12-66***). God gave Solomon the gift of unsurpassed wisdom and riches. Under King Solomon, Israel as a nation was established in greatness and favor world-wide (***1 Kings 10:23-25***).

Now the nature of flesh is that enough is never enough. Flesh has an insatiable desire for more and for the forbidden. In his flesh, Solomon lusted after women. Moreover, he had a particular attraction to the very ones that the Lord had given a strong warning to avoid (***1 Kings 11:1-2***)!

{Dear Father, thank you for another day of growing in truth through Your word. Help me to learn from the ones who have lived before me. I pray to remember that I have a choice—I can choose to walk in Christ's footsteps or to walk in the flesh. I pray to make the choice for Jesus early and often each day. When I keep the Lord first and center, He shows me the pitfalls, the minefields, and the clear path to

*an abundantly rich life. Thank you, Father, for loving me so dearly and showing the way. Thank you that even when I am not willing, You can give me the willingness to be willing (**Philippians 2:13**). I pray for this today. May I keep You at the center in every season of my life! In the name of Jesus I pray. Amen.}*

40.

WHEN FACED WITH PHYSICAL PAIN

Do everything without complaining or arguing, so that you may become blameless and pure, children of God without fault in a crooked and depraved generation, in which you shine like stars in the universe as you hold out the word of life. ~ Philippians 2:14-16

One of the hardest times that I find keeping "murmur-free" is when I am not feeling good physically. When something is hurting in my body, my thoughts seems to go automatically to that pain. I am not always successful in remembering to live out these lessons, but here are some things that have helped me. When I have done them I have been able to rise above my discomfort and be a better witness to those around me:

1. I ask God to take away my pain. I let God know that I *know* that He has the power to miraculously reach down, touch my body and bring the healing that I want. I also let my mouth speak aloud the truth that my healing may not come on this side of heaven—that the choice is His, but I will unashamedly pray for healing today.
2. I ask specific "prayer warriors" to pray for my healing and then, I stop talking about my aches and pains!
3. I pray for the willingness and strength to cooperate with God's treatment program. Healing requires faith, and I pray for the willingness and strength to sincerely do the things that strengthen my faith: I read my Bible. I write out the things I learn. I pray about the things I learn. I play Christian music. I stream in the audible Bible. I listen to recordings of

Bible teachers. I think about how blessed I am to know Jesus and to have been saved!
4. I don't put God to the test (*Matthew 4:7*). I pray for the willingness and strength to do the practical routines that are common sense for good physical and emotional health: adequate rest, moderate exercise, healthy food in healthy amounts, good hydration, daily grooming and hygienic regimes.
5. I call on the Holy Spirit to help me to pour myself into giving unselfishly to another. I make phone calls and I practice listening to the hearts of others. Before ending the call, I pray deeply with them and for them, in the name of Jesus.
6. IF (and only if) I am asked about my condition, I prayerfully tell the truth about the progress of my healing. I then ask for prayers to continue forth in the day murmur-free.

{Dear Father, I pray to never forget that Jesus went through much pain for my freedom. I pray that when I am visited by painful times, that I will keep free from murmuring and complaining. Living in this world is not trouble-free, but each day can be joy-filled and beautiful. I pray to let Your word transform me. I pray to cooperate by yielding to Your program of self-less behavior in the power of the Spirit. It's in the name of Jesus that I pray. Amen.}

41.

ABORTING A RETURN TO SINFUL BEHAVIOR

So I say, let the Holy Spirit guide your lives. Then you won't be doing what your sinful nature craves. ~ Galatians 5:16

If I let my mind wander from the truth, my behavior will soon wander into sin. It is very important that I take my thoughts captive and make them obedient to Christ (**2 Corinthians 10:5**). Here are some practical things that I have found helpful when there seems to be a war raging between my sinful nature and my redeemed heart:

- I expose the attack by telling the Lord what I am feeling and/or what is being said against me. The sooner the better. The more specific, the better. For example I might pray: *{Lord, all of a sudden I feel like crawling into bed. The voices are saying that I don't know what I am doing...that I have bitten off more than I can handle...that I am ALWAYS doing this...}*
- I remind my flesh and the devil that I am a redeemed child of the King: *{Dear Lord, I am your child. I cannot do anything without your help and power. You love me. You will protect me and show me mercy because You love me.}*
- I call on the Holy Spirit to bring forth the sword of the Spirit which is the word of God (**Ephesians 6:17**): *{Please fill me with truth so that I can have the power to be released from all fear. Please flood me with belief in the victory.}*
- I bring to mind Bible verses that I have memorized. (If I can't think of any for my specific attack, I do an internet search for "Bible verses about X") I say the verse aloud and pray the verse aloud. For example: Sometimes I have been afraid to make a phone call to find out information. A verse I have used is **Proverbs 28:1 ~ The wicked man flees though**

no one pursues, but the righteous are as bold as a lion. The prayer that follows might go like this: {*Dear Father, I am no longer wicked because I have been saved by the blood of Jesus. The devil is a "no one" to me now, because I am clothed in the righteousness of Jesus. Please strengthen me to stand firm and to be bold for Jesus! It's in His name that I pray. Amen.*}

- I breathe deeply and I consciously relax the muscles of my body.
- I thank the Lord by saying aloud a prayer of belief: {*I thank you, Father. I thank you. I know You have heard my prayers. I don't know how things are all going to work out, but I KNOW that You know! Thank you for loving me, Lord. Thank you for always being there for me. You are wonderful and I am so grateful that I belong to You.*}
- I take my thoughts away from my feelings and focus on the task at hand. Sometimes it helps to pray aloud: {*This is doable, Lord! This is doable!*} (**Philippians 4:13**)

{*Dear Father, I pray to share clearly and truthfully the things You are teaching me. I pray to keep practicing Your lessons and making them my own. Please keep me out of the food. Please keep me deep in Your word so that my sword is ready for the next attack. It is in the name of Jesus that I pray. Amen.*}

42.

UGLY AND DESPICABLE

No one else so completely sold himself to what was evil in the Lord's sight as Ahab did under the influence of his wife Jezebel. ~ 1 Kings 21:25

King Ahab wanted a certain vineyard near to his house for a vegetable garden. When the owner would not sell it, Ahab pouted, got sullen, and would not eat. When Ahab's wife Jezebel got wind of what was going on, she took matters into her own hands. She cooked up a plan where she got two worthless men to speak against the owner of the vineyard, accusing the owner falsely of cursing God and the king. Afterward, the owner was stoned to death and his land was taken by Ahab (***1 Kings 21:1-16***).

The Bible says in ***1 Kings 21:26*** that Ahab's behavior was as bad as the Amorites before him (whom the Lord had disposed from the Promise Land because of their gross abominations). Though Ahab had done WAY worse things before the vineyard affair, this was the last straw! It caused God to summon Elijah to go to Ahab to let him know that his dynasty would come to a brutal end, in the same way as both Jeroboam and Baasha before him (***1 Kings 21:17-24***).

When a person's heart is not given to the Lord, the flesh steps in and takes control. When flesh is in control, true concern for other people is not a consideration. Moreover, living in the flesh causes the person to become an ugly and despicable specimen of humanity.

*{Dear Father, I pray to remember that I have a choice to either walk with the Spirit or to let the flesh be in control. I pray to live like a child of The Light today (**Philippians 2:14-16**). I pray to be like*

Jesus. Please help me to take the time to hear You speak to my heart through Your word today. I pray for a filling of the Holy Spirit so that I am empowered to do the things that You have asked me to do. Please keep me abstinent and running to You and not to false idols today. Help me to learn a lesson from those who have failed before me. I pray in the name of Jesus Christ. Amen.}

43.

LIVING WATER

"You search the Scriptures, for you believe they give you eternal life. And the Scriptures point to me! Yet you won't come to me so that I can give you this life eternal!

~ John 5:39-40

On the way back to Galilee, Jesus stopped at a well in the Samaritan village of Sychar. The disciples had gone to buy food and Jesus sat wearily at the well waiting. When a woman came to draw water, Jesus asked her for a drink. The woman expressed surprise that He would ask this. She could see that He was a Jew and Jews looked down on Samaritans and would never ask them for a drink (***John 4:1-9***).

Jesus said to her that if she realized who she was talking to, she would be asking Him for living water that would quench her thirst forever. This "Living Water" intrigued the woman so she said to Jesus, "Sir, give me this water." So Jesus told her to go and call her husband to come to the well. When she admitted that she had no husband, Jesus then confronted her with the truth about her adulterous life. As the woman and Jesus continued to talk, she attempted to turn the conversation in another direction. But Jesus kept the conversation deep, not giving in to her attempt to divert the truth (***John 4:10-26***).

Whenever I spend study time in the word, truly asking God again and again to engage my heart, I have an encounter with Jesus like that of the Samaritan woman. My flesh tries desperately to "keep it light", but Jesus draws me in deeper and deeper. Things that I don't think I am ready to deal with are brought out on the table. I am given hope. God shows me that despite my past, He loves me in the present. It is His love which raises me up above all that would attempt to knock me down and bury me under. It is His love that empowers me to keep moving beyond all negativity. It is His love which assures me that He does not play favorites—what He has done for one, He will do for me.

Consistent, heart to heart time in the whole word of God is what Bible immersion is all about. I pray to never stop making this a priority in every day. I pray to never stop teaching others to do the same.

{Dear Father, this is the day that you have made and have given to me. I pray to prize You above all other people, places, and things. You have taught me that when I truly put You first in my day, I don't have to worry about my food or anything else. I pray to continue to bring my thoughts to You. I pray to teach this to others with all the love and skill that You can give me. I pray in the name of Jesus. Amen.}

44.

SADLY MISTAKEN

God opposes the proud but shows favor to the humble.
~ James 4:6

After consulting with his commanders and leaders, David decided to bring the ark of the Lord up from Kiriath-Jearim to Jerusalem, called the city of David. There was a great celebration where Israelites "from the Nile of Egypt to Lebo-hamath" assembled for the festivities (***1 Chronicles 13:5***). Singers and dancers celebrated with instruments and song, and the ark of God was carried in their midst upon a new cart.

When the cart came to a certain threshing floor, the oxen stumbled, and one of the drivers of the cart put out his hand to try to steady the ark. To the shock of everyone, the Lord struck the driver dead for doing this.

David was angered by this act of God, but God knew what He was doing! He was reprimanding David for his presumption. It was a known fact since the time of Moses that the transporting of the ark of God could only be done by the Levites. Though David was king, he still could not treat the sacredness of God outside of the way that was prescribed by God.

This story reminds me of a time in my own life. It was 1985. I was in secular, Twelve Step recovery. I was abstinent, "back-to-back" for about 4 1/2 years. I was sponsoring people. I had started meetings. I had a food plan. I had a fellowship. I had a tool kit of useful living skills—I was working the steps.

I had, what I thought was, a relationship with God. I know now, that because I did not know Jesus as Savior and Lord, I only had a relationship with "a god of my understanding." When the devil returned with a vengeance, I ate again and got very angry with God. But God knew what He was doing. He was exposing my false god.

In order to have eternal life I have to know God as He wants to be known. In order to experience a peaceful, useful, and abundant life on this side of heaven, I have to know how to please God. These things are taught by the Holy Spirit through the word of God.

In light of my compulsive and rebellious nature, it is not enough that I have a shallow interaction with truth. My commitment to being trained by God and practicing the training that He gives, must be intense! I thank the Lord for teaching me how to be immersed in the Bible. I pray for the willingness to remain an eager and consistent student of the word.

{Dear Father, thank you for another day of abstinence and living in the word. Even when I was young I was in the crosshairs of the devil's weapons of annihilation. Thank you for sending Jesus to save me. You are teaching me how to live this life victoriously—not tethered to anyone except the Lord. Please keep me forever abiding in the Lord. I pray to teach others to do the same. It is in the name of Jesus Christ that I pray. Amen.}

45.

HOW TO USE THE BIBLE AS AN INVENTORY TOOL

Search me, God, and know my heart; test me and know my anxious thoughts. See if there is any offensive way in me, and lead me in the way everlasting. ~ Psalm 139:23-24

I try to be vigilant to keep my thoughts clear of negativity, bitterness, fear, anxiety and the like. I try to pray about adverse feelings as soon as they appear—knowing that they can be a gateway to sin. As I consistently "read, study, and apply" with a surrendered and sincere heart, my emotions do not become a problem. But unfortunately, there are times when I have failed to be vigilant and I find myself with a dark cloud hanging over me and I know that it's time for an inventory.

Before I matured in my faith in the Lord Jesus Christ, this would mean days, weeks, and even months of finding the right guide, writing out the questions, finding someone to take my "5th Step", making an appointment, giving my inventory away, and hoping that I had done enough. Today I know that God's word is designed to both uncover the wrong in my life and to bring healing to whatever is going on with me. God's word is designed to bring me back to the foot of the cross and the knowledge that I am deeply loved. Any inventory that does not incorporate Scripture and sincere prayer to the heart of my Savior has proven to be of the type spoken of in ***Proverbs 16:25***.

The Bible has become my ultimate tool for self-reflection and review. It is Spirit-directed and not man-directed. Only the Bible is "God Breathed". It's designed to encourage and equip me as a believer. Its primary focus is on God and not my transgressions, therefore the end result is that I am spurred forward and not weighed down even more.

If you have never used the Bible as an inventory tool, here is a way to begin:

1. Start off with a written letter to the Lord. Be brutally honest with God, without being disrespectful. (The prophet Habakkuk did this very well. See ***Habakkuk 1-4***. Also see many of the Psalms of David).
2. Using your God letter as a cue—identify the overriding emotion.
3. Do an internet search for that emotion. Let's say that the overriding emotion is fear. Then Google "Bible verses about fear."
4. Choose 1 or 2 of the verses, and do a verse study as outlined in the first bullet in most of the "Digging Deeper" sections of the Ninety Days book.
5. Write out a prayer. Include in the prayer what you have learned from the verse study, along with a request for the strength to make the needed changes in your behavior that have been revealed. Pray the written prayer with deep sincerity. (Sometimes I have asked one or two others to pray the prayer with me.)

*{Dear Father, You have taught me that I have often missed out on Your blessings because I have failed to ask You for what I've needed (**James 4:2**). I pray to remember that nothing is impossible for You. You can change me into the likeness of your Son. Help me to keep a close watch on myself and on Your teachings. Please grow my faith and fill me with sober judgement. Keep me from being stunted in my growth by overwhelming emotional strife. Please keep me out of the food and into Your word. I pray in the name of Jesus Christ, my Savior and my Lord. Amen.}*

46.

KEEPING THE RIGHT SIZE

I took you from the pasture, from following the sheep, to be prince over my people Israel. ~ 1 Chronicles 17:7

After things had settled for David, he pondered the fact that he was living in a beautiful home while the ark of God was housed in a tent. Nathan the prophet listened to David and encouraged him to do whatever was in his mind to do about the matter. But later that night, God spoke to Nathan, and told him otherwise. In essence, Nathan was instructed to tell David, "Thanks...but no thanks!" (***1 Chronicles 17:1-15***) David was the king, but he was not the Lord. It was the Lord's decision to determine when a permanent resting place of the ark would be built, and who would build it.

In my flesh it is a natural tendency to forget where the Lord found me and the wreckage that was left behind when I was in control of things. God is God and I am not God. He saved me. I did not save myself. I was the one who could not string two or three days together without eating compulsively. I was the one who fought with depression and low self-esteem. I was the one who felt unloved and forgotten by God. But God in His mercy sought me, found me, and placed my life on The Solid Rock. I am forever grateful, and I pray to keep the right size so that I am not trying to run ahead of God and miss out on even more blessings.

{Dear Father, You have plans for my life and You know what they are. Keep me humbly coming before You throughout the day asking for the next right thing to do. Help me to stay the right size. Before I attempt to do for You, I pray to remember what You have done for me. Your love for me is amazing! I pray that my abstinent life today in the word will bring honor to You. It is in the name of Jesus that I pray. Amen.}

47.

HOW TO HAVE AN ABSTINENT DAY

Anyone who belongs to Christ has become a new person. The old life is gone; a new life has begun! And all of this is a gift from God, who brought us back to himself through Christ. And God has given us this task of reconciling people to him. ~ 2 Corinthians 5:17-18

It is my firm belief today, that if a person is a Christian, then there are two things that are necessary in order to be abstinent day after day. These things are: 1) They must be born again, and 2) They must remember that they are born again!

In the book of John, a Pharisee came to Jesus in the night (***John 3:1-21***). His name was Nicodemus and he was a ruler of the Jews. He was baffled by Jesus and what others (especially his peers) were saying about Him, and he decided to meet with Jesus and find out for himself. He went at night because his closest friends (the other Pharisees) hated Jesus and told the people that Jesus was a phony. Anyone known to follow Jesus would be put out of the synagogue. But Nicodemus just had to know! He said to Jesus, when he came to Him, "No one can do these signs that you do unless God is with him."

What I learned from the story of Nicodemus is that being a Christian is all about being Born Again. And being Born Again is a "Spirit thing" and not a "religious thing". Being born again is not puffing myself up about the many things that I have done for God, but being broken to the heart by the magnificent things that God has done for me!

Because of the sin of Adam and Eve, every one of their children (i.e. the world) has been cut off from an intimate relationship with God. This break was mended when God came down as a man to live a holy life before the world. He became the blood sacrifice for the sin of Adam and Eve. When a human being accepts with his heart this redemption, they become Born Again.

Scripture is a magnificent gift of a loving God. Through Scripture we can know the problem (sin) and remember the solution (Jesus). One who is Born Again comes to love Scripture because it is the story of Jesus Christ, their Savior. Also, one who is Born Again comes to love Scripture because it reminds them that they are in Christ and have been equipped to fight against the adversaries of God.

So, why is it that there are Christians who still struggle with compulsive eating and cannot stay abstinent? My belief is that they are: 1) not Born Again or, 2) they do not remember they are Born Again. To put it another way, they are people who: 1) do not believe what Jesus says about Himself or, 2) they have temporary amnesia, and they run back to their former god of food!

{Dear Father, Your word the Bible is magnificent! Why would I want to keep pursuing any counsel other than Your inerrant word! There is so much to learn. There is so much that You want to teach me. Thank you for giving me a passion to learn from Scripture today. Thank you that I know that the Bible keeps me eye to eye with Jesus and Your will for my life today. May I never forget for one moment that Your will for this day DOES NOT include lusting after food! Please keep me learning and growing through Bible Immersion. Please keep me encouraging others to do the same. It is in the name of Jesus that I pray. Amen.}

48.

THE LIVING, ACTIVE, POWERFUL WORD OF GOD

For the word of God is alive and powerful. It is sharper than the sharpest two-edged sword, cutting between soul and spirit, between joint and marrow. It exposes our innermost thoughts and desires. ~ Hebrews 4:12

For so many years I was a slave to my feelings. If I felt good, I could be a veritable powerhouse—whipping off tasks left and right. If I felt bad, I could bury myself in magazines, television, sleeping, (and of course food)...and it would be a struggle to even get dressed and cleaned up.

I did not know the connection between God's word, my thoughts, and my actions. But the Bible has taught me a very important truth. In **Romans 12:2**, I am reminded that I am transformed by the renewing of my mind. My thoughts and my attitude change when I expose them to truth. I expose my thoughts to truth when I immerse myself into the word of God.

The exercise of reading, studying, and applying the word of God, works better than a therapy session for me. God is teaching me that He speaks to me in His word. **2 Timothy 3:16-17** tells me that His word teaches me, trains me, and equips me for all the things that I encounter in my day to day life.

{Dear Father, thank you for the willingness to put meeting with You at the top of this day. Please help me to remember that my thoughts will influence my attitudes and feelings. Keep me running to Your word today when I feel off and overwhelmed. Keep me digging deeper and praying about the insights that You reveal, as I pursue

*You in this way. Thank you, Lord, because being immersed in your word has given me a special added bonus. Your word has become hands-down, better than any food that I have ever known! You are showing me the path of life (**Psalm 16:11**). I pray to stay rooted in Your word forever. It is in the name of Jesus Christ that I pray. Amen.}*

49.

WHEN THE GOINGS GET TOUGH

He set to work resolutely and built up all the wall that was broken down and raised towers upon it, and outside it he built another wall, and he strengthened the Millo in the city of David. He also made weapons and shields in abundance. ~ 2 Chronicles 32:5

When life gets tough, the devil tempts my flesh to pull back and engage in some form of "poor me" behavior. I usually feel VERY sleepy, or I have this urge to go buy something. Self-care devil-style, is always in the order of "you-deserve-a-break-today"! Self-care, God's ways is to get going—pulling closer to Him and using the tools He has given to me to stand my ground. King Hezekiah is an excellent example of the "tough getting going when the goings get tough."

The Bible says that King Hezekiah worked hard to undo all the despicable things his father had done to bring sin to Judah. But after he had spent many years doing these wonderful things for the Lord, the king of Assyria encamped around Judah with the intention of conquering it and taking it for himself.

Hezekiah could have gotten on the "pity potty" and given up. Instead, he got into action. He built up the broken walls, made weapons and shields in abundance, and gathered the people together for encouragement. Moreover, he met with the prophet Isaiah and they stormed the gates of heaven in prayer.

God heard the prayers of His servants and He put Sennacherib of Assyria to shame. He sent the angel of the Lord into Sennacherib's camp and killed 185,000 of his soldiers. Defeated, Sennacherib returned to Nineveh (***Isaiah 37:36-38***).

*{Dear Father, thank you for another day of abstinence and being immersed in Your word. Please help me to remember that I have been reborn and that You have not given me a spirit of fear, but a spirit of power and love and of self-discipline (**2 Timothy 1:7**). Give me the courage to stand firm in my faith. Keep me prayerful and trusting that at the exact right time You will supply all that I need for success—including affirmation and reward. You want the best for me and doing life your way is always the best. It's in the name of Jesus I pray. Amen.}*

50.

VERSES AND PRAYERS TO FIGHT DISCOURAGEMENT

He said: "Listen, King Jehoshaphat and all who live in Judah and Jerusalem! This is what the LORD says to you: 'Do not be afraid or discouraged because of this vast army. For the battle is not yours, but God's.~ 2 Chronicles 20:15

Discouragement is one of the favorite tools of the devil. As Christians we can be moving along at a steady pace and one thought or one incident can send us spinning. We can feel confused, lost, and on our own. We forget that we are not our flesh and we start to behave in ways that are not in keeping with the New Creations that we are.

One of the best ways that I know to break this downward spiral is reading scripture and then praying scripture back to the heart of God. Here are some verses and prayers that can help you if you are presently in a place of discouragement:

1. ***1 Corinthians 15:58 ~ My dear brothers and sisters, stand firm. Let nothing move you. Always give yourselves fully to the work of the Lord, because you know that your labor in the Lord is not in vain.*** *{Dear Father, I pray to remember that negativity is not from You. Negativity is designed to stop me in my tracks and veer me off the goals that You have for me today. Strengthen me, Lord. Help me to set my face like a flint. Help me to never forget that You know my heart and nothing that I do for You is done in vain.}*
2. ***Proverbs 3:5-6 ~ Trust in the LORD with all your heart; and lean not unto your own understanding. In all your ways acknowledge him, and he shall direct your paths.*** *{Dear Father, I belong to Jesus now. He is my Lord. He is my director. Please*

fill my heart with this truth. Even when I don't fully understand how to make things work out, I pray to remember that You DO know how to work things out successfully. I pray to remember Your word. I pray to submit to Your will. And I thank you right now for the glorious outcome that is on the way.}

3. **Joshua 1:9 ~ Have not I commanded you? Be strong and of good courage; be not afraid, neither be you dismayed: for the LORD your God is with you wherever you go.** *{Dear Father, I pray to remember Your anointing and Your call on my life. There are captives that need to be set free. There are blind ones who are crying out to see again. There is a world around me that is perishing for lack of knowing the Good News of Jesus Christ. Bring back to my mind the lessons You have taught me in your word. Fill me with the Holy Spirit so that I can rise above my feelings and walk out boldly in your truth.}*

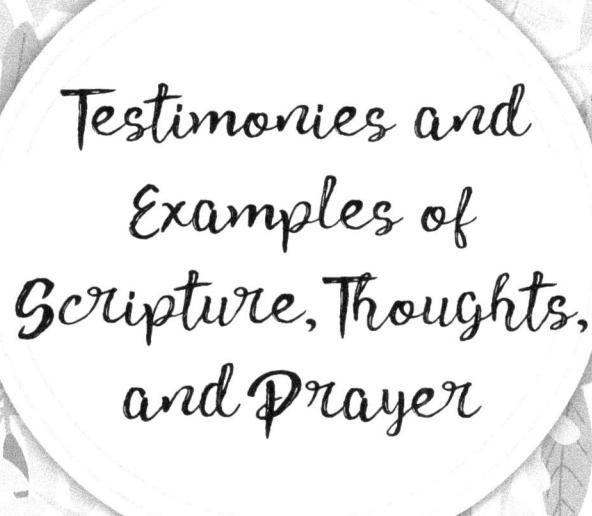

Testimonies and Examples of Scripture, Thoughts, and Prayer

Ellen, New York

Bible Immersion is helping me to start my day in God's word through prayer, study, meditation, and writing. Because of Bible Immersion I am spending more time with my Lord. It is building my structure and making me stronger in Scripture. I am truly thankful for being taught this way. May God continue to use all of us to help people and bring Him glory.

Scripture, Thoughts, and Prayer
Matthew 16:24 ~ A disciple is not above his teacher, nor a servant above his master.

- A servant obeys his master, so stay in your lane!
- Do not be afraid of those who kill the body, but cannot kill the soul; rather, be afraid of the one who can destroy both soul and body in hell.
- *{Lord, I understand the enemy comes to steal, kill, and destroy. He does all that, but he cannot kill my soul. I am not afraid of him. But I do fear YOU, Father God. I am so grateful for your word. It is making me stronger in you. Please be my feast today. In the name of Jesus I pray. Amen.}*

Eunice, Ohio

I have been a student of the Bible for over 35 years. I have also read my Bible consistently over the years. I have been using the Bible Immersion method of study for over a year. Bible Immersion has taken me to deeper depths and higher heights in God's word. Because of this technique I am seeing the Scriptures in a new light and I understand the Scriptures more.

Two or three times a week, I share with other believers who are using the Bible Immersion method of study. Being able to discuss my writings and hear the writings of others has reinforced God's word in my spirit and mind.

Scripture, Thoughts, and Prayer
Hebrews 3:6 (NLT) ~ But Christ, as the Son, is in charge of God's entire house. And we are God's house, if we keep our courage and remain confident in our hope in Christ.

- I think Paul is talking about keeping our courage in believing in the finished work of Jesus Christ. We have to stay courageous when the devil tries to use the news and other horrors of this world to make us feel fearful, hopeless, and helpless.
- God might be saying that He has ALL power, so there is no need to fear. Put our hope in Him. We have His power—Holy Spirit Power. We have the power of prayer, praise, love, and believing!
- *{Dear Father God, Lord Jesus, Holy Spirit, thank you for being the Living God with ALL power! You are ALL knowing and everywhere ALL the time. In Jesus Name, I give thanks and pray. Amen.}*

Carrie, Washington

Bible Immersion is like opening up a gift each morning with a surprise inside just for me from the Lord! Knowing I am focusing on hearing from the Lord and asking Him to connect my heart with His heart gives me peace and assurance that I will hear from Him. I know that He will help me grow spiritually and increase my faith as He gives peace, conviction, and guidance, according to my need!

To do Bible Immersion, I get up, head to my Bible, notebook and iPad. I check my email to get the reading and the audio link, and off

I go. This new-found, deeper connection with the Lord motivates me to share about Bible Immersion. It is exciting and hard to keep it to myself. I have taught it to others…even my grandchildren!

Scripture, Thoughts, and Prayer
Genesis 27:42b ~ … Esau is 'consoling himself' concerning you (Jacob) by planning to kill you…

- Oh, how we try to 'console ourselves' with food, revenge, etc.
- Only God can truly console me!
- *{Lord, Your words have jumped off the page! You know my present struggle with a situation that has brought bitterness, resentment and the need to forgive. Please allow me to let go of all the bitterness, etc. and only 'console myself' with You and Your word.}*

Tammy, Georgia

When I first came to the Bible for Food Ministry, I was desperate from a progressive 5 year relapse into compulsive overeating. Despite all I tried, I could not even get 5 days of freedom from the misery of binge eating!

As I listened on phone meetings I was taught to make sure that I put an ample amount of Scripture into my heart each day. I was reminded that the Bible is "powerful and active" (***Hebrews 4:12***) and would cause a transformation through the instilling of truth (***Romans 12:2***).

At one of the Bible for Food retreats, I got to practice Bible Immersion and meet other people in the ministry. I began praying with them and establishing close relationships with them. I am grateful to say that I got my abstinence back! I feel so blessed now to have this fellowship of believers to pray with and to support me with my Achilles heel, which has always been the food!

Scripture, Thoughts, and Prayer
2 Corinthians 10:5 ~ We demolish arguments and every pretension that sets itself up against the knowledge of God, and we take captive every thought to make it obedient to Christ.

- Sinful and lustful thoughts will come to try to make us think we're powerless to sin and make us go back to old behaviors; however, we are able to take control of these thoughts with God's word.
- God's word helps us to recognize what is true and what is untrue.
- Every time a "food thought" comes, I start reciting God's word. Scripture empowers me to realize that sin is no longer my master, and the desire to eat will leave if I just give it a little time.
- *{Dear Heavenly Father, thank you so much for Your love, Your word, and the Holy Spirit which enables me to act according to Your will and delivers me from sin. I pray that I will continue to know who I am in Christ every day so that I can stay abstinent and be a witness to others of Your power, grace and mercy. I pray to bring glory to You. In Jesus Name. Amen.}*

※ ※ ※ ※ ※ ※

Dawn, Massachusetts

I like Bible Immersion because it changes my spirit, my attitude, my thinking, and my fear. Bible Immersion puts the word of God into me and gives me a whole new perspective on life.

Scripture, Thoughts, and Prayer
Genesis 39:1 ~ Now Joseph had been taken down to Egypt. Potiphar, an Egyptian who was one of Pharaoh's officials, the captain of the guard, bought him from the Ishmaelites who had taken him there.

- *(39:2)… The Lord was with Joseph so that he prospered* …In my own life, I know this to be true. I am so in need of the

Lord. I need Him every day—morning, afternoon, evening. I am nothing without Him!
- ***(39:4)… Potiphar put him in charge of his household, and he entrusted to his care everything he owned***…My boss gave me the check book to the store, the important keys, and the passwords to the computers while he was away. I know he trusts me.
- ***(39:5)…the LORD blessed the household of the Egyptian because of Joseph***…I want to follow the Lord as Joseph did. All the days of my life!
- *{Dear Father, I always had a special place in my heart for Joseph. I want to be good. I want to obey You. I am in need of Your help. Thank you, Lord, for helping me to grow. Thank you for my marriage. Thank you for healing me with Your teaching word, one day at a time. I love you, Lord.}*

※ ※ ※ ※ ※ ※

Annette, Texas

I know how important it is for me to read, study and apply God's word. I go straight to God's word most mornings because I know if I do not, my day won't start out right.

Bible Immersion has taught me how to *really* study God's word. When I journal scriptures, thoughts and prayers I am reminded of the truth and this helps me keep a proper perspective of who I belong to. I am a child of God!

Scripture, Thoughts, and Prayer
Matthew 25:32, 40 ~ All the nations will be gathered before Him and He will separate the people one from another as a shepherd separates the sheep and the goats…The King will reply, "I tell you the truth, whatever you did for one of the least of these brothers of mine, you did for me also.

- I know that through Jesus' blood I am a sheep. I will sit at the Lord's right hand.
- I will not be treated as a goat. I will not be separated from the Lord.
- However, I have a need to be more of a servant for Jesus. I need to work for the Lord in an area of service to others.
- If there is a need, then I want to be available. I want to step out of my comfort zone.
- *{Dear Lord, I cannot possibly do any of this without Your help. I am seeing it clearer; however I still don't know where I belong. Help me to stay focused on You and what it is You are telling me to do. Forgive me for my inattentiveness to you. Forgive me if my opportunities come and go and I stand still. Help me in this earthly body that is so imperfect, to press forward anyway and to let you direct me. No more acting like a goat. Teach me what I need to know to serve. Help me when I'm afraid. I know I will face obstacles along the way. May they not distract me. I ask all of these things in Jesus Christ's name. Amen.}*

※ ※ ※ ※ ※ ※

Kim, Georgia

Bible Immersion has changed my life. Prior to immersing myself in God's word, I walked around with a feeling of emptiness. It wasn't until I went through the Ninety Days of Encouragement book, and began reading the Bible daily that I realized what that emptiness was. By the grace of God, today my life is full. I know God's love, joy, and peace. Today Jesus my Lord and Savior fills the emptiness that I felt for so long.

Scripture, Thoughts, and Prayer
Exodus 1:16 But the midwives feared God, and did not do as the king of Egypt had commanded them, but let the boys live.

- The midwives knew that God had forbidden murder. They chose to obey God and not the king of Egypt.
- I am to obey God and not man.
- It's important that I look at my people pleasing.
- My desire is to be obedient and pleasing to the Lord and not to be seeking approval of others.
- *{Father, I pray to make right choices. I pray to be in Your word daily so that I know right from wrong. Lord, I want to be pleasing and obedient to You in every area of my life. Please lead, guide, and direct me. It's in Jesus' name that I pray. Amen.}*

Danielle, New York

Bible Immersion has stretched me to dig deeper in my faith. I now have a fellowship of other believers who are also in the word. They lift me up and they remind me of what the Bible teaches. This helps me stay in the will of God more each day.

From Genesis, I have learned how the world started. I now understand why Jesus had to come for us. It is making so much sense and "making sense" is causing the truth to shine ever brighter in my heart!

Bible Immersion is providing a structure. Each morning I am learning to make the word one of the first things I do. A solid foundation is being laid daily as I feel the Lord speaking personally to me. Each day I am shown something that I never saw before!

I keep hearing, "Be faithful in the small things and I will be faithful in the big things." That is why even when I do not feel like immersing in the word, I do it anyway. I now realize that I am not fighting flesh, I am in a spiritual battle. I truly see from doing Bible Immersion, that I must put on "the full armor of God"!

Dorothea, New York

Bible Immersion has rekindled my love for the study of God's word. It has drawn me closer to God and increased my faith as well. Now I run to the word of God when sticky situations arise. I go to my knees, open my Bible and see what God has to say to me about the matter. For me, Bible Immersion is not a chore, but a delight. I look forward to it each day!

Scripture, Thoughts, and Prayer
Exodus 15:27 (NIV) ~ Then they came to Elim, where there were twelve springs and seventy palm trees, and they camped there near the water.

- The Lord led the Israelites to Elim where there was plenty of water and shade. But before they arrived in Elim, they were led to the Dessert of Shur (*15:22*) where they endured three days without water. Moses cried to the Lord, and God supplied water for them in the dessert (*15:25*) . Still, the Israelites had to endure the tough time in Shur before they could enjoy the refreshing time in Elim.
- God is saying to me that He is going to allow dry times, tough times, lean times in my life to test me to see what is in my heart.
- He wants to expose and clean out the junk in my heart such as impatience and fear. He wants to build me up!
- Will I grumble, complain, or cry "Where is God!" during these tests like the Israelites did? Or will I stand in faith trusting that God will keep me during the highs and lows of life!
- *{Lord, I have often failed this test. I have grumbled and complained when things got rough. Thank you that You have kept me abstinent by Your grace. Still, in addition to abstinence, I desire to have a better attitude during trials. Help me to grow up in my trust and faith in you. Thank you for the changes I do*

see. Still I desire more. Thank you Lord. I love You because You first loved me. In Jesus name I pray. Amen.}

❧ ❧ ❧ ❧ ❧ ❧

Deanna, Florida

I have been a Christian since the age of 6, and have loved the Lord and His word all this time. I learned about Bible Immersion when I got involved in Bible for Food. I witnessed the transformation of one of the young ladies in the group through Bible immersion. It was then that I decided to embrace this new way of reading and studying the scriptures, too. Today I can say that I not only like Bible Immersion….I love it!

Bible Immersion has caused my daily time in God's word to be more consistent. I have been encouraged to be in His word the first thing in the morning, and at night. It has been like a fresh kiss from the Lord when I wake up. And at night, it is as if His precious word is tucking me into bed.

Bible Immersion surrounds me with others who are also serious about God's word. I don't feel alone. Either through the meetings, outreach calls, the shepherding program or the recorded messages online, I can reinforce this discipline and the insights I am receiving.

Most recently I have started practicing the suggestion of playing an audio version of the scripture while I read the scripture. This has helped with distractions and retention.

Please understand, I don't do Bible Immersion perfectly and I do miss some readings. But I do as I have been told and don't try to catch up. I just jump into the reading of the day—knowing that the Lord honors my desire to know Him. The intimacy I have with Him and the wisdom from Him is indescribable!

If you are tired of living the way you are, try another way. Try Bible Immersion. It is well worth it!

❀ ❀ ❀ ❀ ❀ ❀

Dorothea, California

I learned about Bible immersion and Bible for Food in April 2017 and my life has changed. I look forward every day to having my personal time with the Lord. I feel He speaks directly to me. I learned the following from listening, underlining, journaling and praying.

Scripture, Thoughts, and Prayer
Matthew 12:43 ~ "When a defiling evil spirit is expelled from someone, it drifts along through the desert looking for an oasis, some unsuspecting soul it can bedevil. When it doesn't find anyone, it says, 'I'll go back to my old haunt. 'On return it finds the person spotlessly clean, but vacant. It then runs out and rounds up seven other spirits more evil than itself and they all move in, whooping it up. That person ends up far worse off than if he'd never gotten cleaned up in the first place.

- The person thought he had all the junk cleared out but he had failed to enlarge his spiritual life. He was not ready for God.
- I understand this passage more. We have to fill up the empty places with God's word and continue to enlarge our spiritual life.
- I have had many deliverances and have been set free from many addictions but I was not immersing myself in the word of God. This had been a pattern for me for 38+ years.
- *{I thank you Lord God for revealing truth to me. I pray, dear Lord, that I will continue to make You number one in my life. I pray that I will continue to be immersed in the word of God and that the Bible will be my food. Thank you God. In the name of Jesus I pray. Amen.}*

Matthew 8:34 ~ Those who heard about it were angry about the drowned pigs. A mob formed and demanded that Jesus get out and not come back.

- They were mad about the drowned pigs. They cared more about the animals than people.
- They wanted Jesus to leave and they demanded that he go.
- *{Dear Lord Jesus, I never want to be blind and to care more about insignificant people places and things. I want to be aware of Your presence at all times. I never want to tell You to leave. Please, Lord, keep me 100% focused on You. It's in your name I pray. Amen}.*

🙏🙏🙏🙏🙏🙏

Sherri, New Jersey

I learned about Bible Immersion through Bible for Food. I came to Bible for Food because of the peace I heard and saw in the teacher. I had been searching to know the Lord, yet never looked for answers in the Bible. I looked in 12-step literature and meetings, and books about the Lord—everything but the Word of the Lord, the Bible. Bible Immersion has helped me read and understand the Word in a way that is personal and memorable. I look forward to it like I used to look forward to bingeing on food.

Scripture fills my soul. Every morning I look forward to reading the Old and New Testament and seeing how it relates to my life and thoughts. I look to the Word to solve my problems because it is the love story and instruction manual of the Lord.

Scripture, Thoughts, and Prayer
Matthew 10:34 "Do not suppose that I have come to bring peace to the earth. I did not come to bring peace, but a sword."

- The material world is full of evil due to original sin and our sinful nature. There will be suffering and struggle and the Word is my weapon.
- The Word is active and sharp and will arm me for battle against the enemy, Satan. My battle is not with people, but with Satan.
- *{I pray not to fight evil with evil or seek revenge. Revenge belongs to You. I pray to stay strong in the Word and fortify myself with faith. I pray to do Your work by living the Word and carrying Your message of salvation. Amen.}*

Bridget, Hawaii

Bible Immersion has changed my life. Through it I have learned about the true character of God. As a result, I am able to love God more and to trust Him—my faith has been indescribably strengthened! I credit Bible Immersion for helping me to stay abstinent for over 2 years at the time of this writing. This is my longest, continuous stretch of abstinence ever.

Bible Immersion has enabled me to hear God's instructions for my life and obey them. He equips me through His word to live this life as He has intended. When I walk along His paths, I wind up at amazing destinations. When I walk my own path, I wind up in dark, scary, unfulfilling, unrewarding, and empty-promise destinations. God's promises are never empty, but filled with abundance.

Scripture, Thoughts, and Prayer
Genesis 45:7-8"And God sent me before you to preserve for you a remnant on earth, and to keep alive for you many survivors. So, it was not you who sent me here, but God.

- Joseph was telling his brothers it was ok they had sold him into slavery. He recognized God's greater purpose was at work in

the midst of his suffering - to fulfill God's promise to Abraham to multiply his descendants, make them numerous as the stars.
- Joseph wound up saving his family during the time of famine. God's promise to Abraham couldn't have been fulfilled if his lineage was not kept alive, nor could Jesus, a descendant of Judah, Joseph's brother, have lived if Judah had died in the famine.
- I must look for the greater purpose of God in the midst of struggles. This alone brings me peace and joy in the midst of sorrow. I know that I am loved and cared for by the Lord despite the appearance of my earthly circumstances.
- ***Romans 8:28 ~ "And we know that in all things God works for the good of those who love him, who have been called according to his purpose."***
- *{Dear Father God, thank you for Your word, for who You are, and for Your love for me. Please help me to look for Your greater purpose in the midst of my struggles, to see that You have sent me here for a specific calling and purpose to serve You. Help me see and obey that calling today Lord. I pray all this in Your name, Jesus. Amen.}*

🌿🌿🌿 🌿🌿🌿

April, New York

I have been maintaining my abstinence for over 30 years. Several years ago I began using Bible Immersion and its practice of underlining, selecting and exploring scripture (the "USE" technique). Bible Immersion has transformed my life!

One of the most significant changes that I have noticed is the stabilizing of my emotions. Difficulties in coping with my feelings have always played a huge part in my misbehavior with the food, and with my interpersonal relationships. I would calm my emotions by either running to people or running to food. Once I put the food down, running to people became my drug of choice. Today, God's word is changing this. I am growing in the knowledge of who I am in Christ. His word is giving me the courage to do things that I have never done before.

Bible Immersion is a discipline that I do at the beginning of my day. I have learned to give God the "first fruits". I used to never set my alarm, but one day at a time I do. If I am going through a particularly challenging time, I stay even longer immersing in the word. I do more writing, more praying, and more searching the Scriptures. It takes time. But I do it anyway! It is very hard to explain the transformation that takes place when I finish. All I know is that I feel better and I am ready to face my day.

Scripture, Thoughts, and Prayer
Philippians 4:6-7 do not be anxious about anything, but in everything by prayer and supplication with thanksgiving let your requests be made known to God. 7 And the peace of God, which surpasses all understanding, will guard your hearts and your minds in Christ Jesus.

- The emotion of fear has always been a spirit that has tormented me most of my life.
- It has been a ferocious voice from the enemy attacking my mind with horrific lies about me, my circumstances, and people.
- This scripture calms me down by telling me to not be fearful, but to pray! To pray—to pour my heart out to the Lord about all my fears. About everything!
- *{Dear Papa, thank you for Your Word today! It is my hope! You are my hope! You are my strength! Help me to not be afraid of anything. Help me to put my trust in You and believe You when you tell me that You will never leave me or forsake me (**Hebrews 13:5**). Lo, You are with me always even till the end of the age (**Matthew 28:20**). Papa, please help me when the enemy starts attacking me with lies in my mind. Take the thoughts captive and replace them with your Truth (**2 Corinthians 10:4-5**). In Jesus Name. Amen.}*

Drena, Maryland

It took me almost fifty years to admit that I was an alcoholic. I always believed in God, but I did not have a personal relationship with my Lord and Savior Jesus Christ. Knowing that I needed help, I joined Celebrate Recovery, a program based on the eight principles from the Beatitudes. This program helped me to know Jesus, and that His word was the only way I could be delivered from my hurts, habits and hang ups.

I was very familiar with the verse "Honor your body as the temple of the Holy Spirit," but I didn't really understand what it meant. It wasn't until I attended a Bible for Food retreat that I understood that I was dishonoring God by going to the food instead of Him. When I went to food when I was lonely, fearful, stressed, or dealing with issues of low self-esteem, it took me some time to realize that this was an abomination.

The *Ninety Days: Encouragement for the Christian Overeater* book and the Bible Immersion technique helped me to learn who my God is. I thank God that this is the fifth year of being committed to reading the entire Bible in a year. These readings helped me to really know who God is and experience His unfailing love for me. Everything that I could possibly need is in my Abba Father!

Scripture, Thoughts, and Prayer
Psalm 8:1~ "O LORD, our Lord, how excellent is Your name in all the earth.

- I praise God because He is everything that I could ever need.
- This Scripture is especially relevant during this time of healing from my surgery. He made a way for me to get the best care and services.

- He provided me with a support system that took care of things I could not do for myself.
- *{Dear Father, I could not thank You enough for being everything I needed!}*

※ ※ ※ ※ ※ ※

Debbie, Indiana

Bible Immersion has helped me to get excited again about reading God's word. It has renewed my faith in that I can hear Him speak to me personally.

I have been taught through my church how important it is to get up every morning and get in the word. Bible Immersion has given me a technique that has helped me to finish my reading with my head lifted up and my heart filled with hope!

Bible Immersion is helping me to get free from the false idols in my life and is helping me to grow in my relationship with Jesus Christ.

Scripture, Thoughts, and Prayer
Matthew 16:24 ~ Then Jesus said to his disciples, "If anyone desires to come after me, let him deny himself and take up his cross and follow me."

- I have a sin nature that is more mindful of self rather than God and others.
- My flesh seeks to please self rather than God.
- I died with Christ and I no longer live.
- I need to die to anything that is drawing me away from Jesus.
- *{Dear Father, I have to die to self if I want to follow Jesus. Please help me to deny myself so I can truly follow Him. In the name of Jesus I pray. Amen.}*

Kathleen, California

Bible Immersion is an amazing, uplifting blessing! I learned about Bible Immersion from a friend who had attended a Bible for Food spring retreat.

I began my own journey by searching God's word. Each morning I kept several journals—what God was teaching me, questions I had for God, and prayers.

Some months later I had the opportunity to attend a retreat myself. There I was instructed to add the auditory modality to my Bible reading. I was exposed to Bible Gateway.com and their free library of audio Bibles in many translations. I can't even begin to describe the amazing experience of listening and reading along in Scripture, while inviting the Holy Spirit to teach me! I feel inspired and set free one day at a time.

An added bonus to my personal study time is that I am now on the same one-year Bible reading schedule as others who use Bible Immersion. Studying the same passage allows for discussion and a deeper level of conversation about God's Word. We share what we learn from the Lord's teachings, and from the Holy Spirit's nudging. It is a practice that I intend to continue all my living days.

Sharon, Virginia

There are so many wonderful promises and instructions found in the word of God. The Bible reminds me to taste and see that the LORD is good! (***Psalm 34:8***)

I commit to reading, meditating, and praying on what I read. I am then able to stand on God's word. I need this kind of renewal daily—sometimes multiple times in my day.

Scripture, Thoughts, and Prayer
John 1:1 ~ In the beginning was the Word, and the Word was with God, and the Word was God.

- Jesus Christ my Savior, Lord, and King, is the Living Word.
- Jesus Christ is alive eternally. Therefore, the Bible which is the written Word is alive.
- The Bible is a manual for love-filled, righteous living on this earth.
- *{Dear Father, I am blessed to know this Living Lord. Thank you for the Bible that keeps me living in the world, but not being "of" the world. In the name of Jesus I pray. Amen.}*

※ ※ ※ ※ ※ ※

Mindy, California

Reading the Bible daily and employing Bible Immersion allows God's Word to strengthen and guide me through every challenge. God's word reminds me that as a believer in Christ and of the ancestry of Abraham, I have a powerful spiritual DNA. I can do all things in Christ because He strengthens me. I fellowship with Him and share my heart, and He ministers back to me through His presence and great love.

Scripture, Thoughts, and Prayer
Exodus 35:1-2: Then Moses called together the whole community of Israel and told them, "These are the instructions the Lord has commanded you to follow. You have six days each week for your ordinary work, but the seventh day must be a Sabbath day of complete rest, a holy day dedicated to the Lord."

- There is a holy rest that is literally rest! How glorious! This went for the whole community. Lack of this holy rest would affect the community and vice versa.
- There is a delicate balance necessary to be a good steward of my physical body to house the precious gift of God's spirit. Eating too heavy or too light, and turning to either of the two for "rest", causes confusion even on a molecular level.
- There is a season for everything (***Ecclesiastes 3:1-11***). Too much or not enough "quiet time with God," exercise, food, fellowship, sleep, work, etc., can throw everything off. The imbalance is sometimes caused by my ego to achieve OR the opposite.
- I run away from what I am supposed to be doing because I'm afraid I won't be good enough and/or the discomfort involved in the work will be too much to bear.
- Sometimes I'm plain exhausted to the point of being dizzy or faint and I wonder if I can accomplish what "I think" is being required of me, and then I resent a whole "community."
- I've been disillusioned by perfection because I compared myself to someone's outsides and perfection was never required of me in the first place!
- *{Lord, I'm overwhelmed! Help me to know my role in the many communities you have placed me in --the Body of Christ, as a wife, mother, Assistant, Psalmist, Friend, Church Member, etc-- I just want to please YOU. Help me to know the days of rest and the days of work. You said that those who labor should come to You for help. Help me to cast my cares on You in the midst of work. You sacrificed your Son for me. I will reverence this rest in You as I continue in my gift of righteousness through Yeshua's shed blood. My life matters. I will rest in You and preserve my health. You are so loving and gentle and there is no condemnation in You. Help me to remember that as I go about my day.}*

Patricia, Maryland

I like Bible Immersion because when using it the Bible comes alive and speaks directly to me regarding my present, past, or upcoming situations. Listening and reading simultaneously has shown me how easy it is to read through the Bible in a year. Bible Immersion has challenged and encouraged me to have a daily, consistent, quality time with the Lord.

Scripture, Thoughts, and Prayer
Zechariah 10:5, 12 ~ They will be like mighty warriors in battle, trampling their enemies in the mud under their feet. Since the LORD is with them as they fight, they will overthrow even the enemy's horsemen… By my power I will make my people strong, and by my authority they will go wherever they wish. I, the LORD, have spoken!"

- For a very long time I have been battling the food addiction issue. I have used food incorrectly for far too long. It is a struggle to "consistently" not overeat, not eat compulsively, and not eat under stress.
- God's word reminds me that the Lord is with me as I fight, and that I WILL overthrow the enemy!
- I am reminded of God's power and the ability that it gives me to overcome. Nevertheless, it is my choice whether I choose to believe and to obey God.
- I am determined today to live for God and living for God does not include gluttony!
- With that said, victory requires that I trust Him with my life, with my choices, and with the endeavors I have set out to accomplish.
- God has given me so much that is good, and that He wants to use for His glory. The discipline with the food must be dealt with and I am dealing with it!

- *{Father, every day I actively confront this issue. Some days I am victorious and other days I am defeated. This struggle with the food is a monster because I have often chosen to fight it inconsistently. Help me to stand firm—knowing You are with me. Help me not to refuse Your help when You come to my aide. I thank You in advance, knowing that You have already given me the power to win this battle once and for all! In Jesus' Name I pray. Amen.}*

Meechie, Maryland

I enjoy Bible Immersion because it has disciplined me to want to search the Scriptures. The Word becomes so ALIVE to me. When I practice Bible Immersion I love how the Holy Spirit speaks to me and reveals what He is saying to me through His Word!

Scripture, Thoughts, and Prayer
Micah 6:3-4, 5b, 8 (NIV) ~ "My people, what have I done to you? How have I burdened you? Answer me. I brought you up out of Egypt and redeemed you from the land of slavery. I sent Moses to lead you, also Aaron and Miriam. ...Remember your journey from Shittim to Gilgal, that you may know the righteous acts of the Lord...He has shown you, O mortal, what is good. And what does the Lord require of you? To act justly and to love mercy and to walk humbly with your God."

- The way I've treated God is a shame! I cannot recall how many times I've called out to God and then turned my back on Him.
- He's brought me out of dangerous situations that I had placed myself in. He even sent the Word to me which I rejected. In a short time, I was back to my sinful ways—another situation, another bailout, another situation, another bailout...repeat!

- However, during one specific situation, He humbled me. From that moment, I began to see Him working in the midst of my woes, and proclaimed His marvelous acts and mercy towards me.
- Now, I know better! Now, I lift my eyes to the Lord, the Creator, Who helps me (***Psalm 121***). And because He knows me by name, He watches over me, and He protects me.
- *{Thank you Lord for loving me in my mess!! More importantly, thank you for cleansing me! You love me so much to pursue me-- then and now! You've given me eyes to see Your Goodness and ears to receive Your Divine Words of encouragement, peace, truth, and wisdom. Even though I don't deserve it, I ask that You keep Your Righteous Hand over me. Amen!}*

※ ※ ※ ※ ※ ※

Jasmine, Washington D.C.

Bible immersion is helping me to take the word and apply it to where I am in my life. I am learning to approach the word with anticipation and to channel my emotions in a healthy way. I am being given divine instructions on how to navigate through my day successfully.

Scripture, Thoughts, and Prayer
Genesis 16:9 ~ The angel of the LORD said to her, "Return to your mistress and submit to her."

- Submit to your authority even in your distress; during hardship don't run (God hears).

Genesis 16:13 ~ Thereafter, Hagar used another name to refer to the Lord, who had spoken to her. She said, "You are the God who sees me."

- God sees (el Roi). I don't have to worry when I'm faced with situations that are not right and beyond my control because God sees.
- Beer-lahai-roi ("well of the living one who sees")—stay at the well!
- *{Lord, help me to submit to those in authority, even when I am not being treated fairly. Help me to respond in ways that say, " I know that God sees and cares how I respond." Help me to give my hurt over to You and not seek relief in things that may not be healthy. Show me how and when to rest when I'm feeling overwhelmed. I thank you for entrusting me with hardships so that when I make it through, I can be a helpful example to others. I thank you for being a real and present God to help me in my time of need. In Jesus' Name. Amen.}*

Laura, New York

Daily Bible Immersion blesses me. I am able to maintain a spiritual fitness that empowers me to face life on life's terms. I am learning to turn to the One true God, and not to things outside of Him. In this daily time of immersing in the word I am emptied of self so that I can be led by God. I am enabled to be rightly related to God and to others.

Through daily Bible Immersion I experience being healthy, holy, humble, helpful, honest, and happy. I am learning to enjoy the people in my life and to bring enjoyment to them.

Scripture, Thoughts, Prayer
Matthew 21:32 ~ For John came to you in the way of righteousness, and you did not believe him, but the tax collectors and the prostitutes believed him and even when you saw it, you did not afterward change your minds and believe him.

- Many are told about God at a young age. They grow up in Christian homes, but when released to make their own choices, they choose to go their own way.
- Some neither know God, nor hear about Him. They get mad when they are in poverty and struggle for too long. They were never lead to read the Bible daily. They never experienced Christian Discipleship. They never learned how to walk in His ways and what their part is in their relationship with God.
- Two different groups, yet they both made the decision to do things their own way. They engaged in sinful behavior—lying, cheating, stealing, adultery, sexual promiscuity, drinking, drugging, spending, overeating, etc. They found themselves suffering, as well as causing others to stumble and suffer because of their choices.
- But like the prostitute and tax collector, they turned to God with their whole heart and He welcomed them into His Kingdom!
- *{Father God, thank you that You are a forgiving Father. Thank You for Your steadfast love, faithfulness, and mercy. Father, I ask You, please help me to never go astray again! Please help others to believe—my family members, friends, and co-workers who do not know You, or who think they know You, but are really going their own way. Please help still others who know You, but are mad at You. Please give them the desire to turn to You, read Your Word daily, and experience coming into Your Kingdom and wanting to serve You. In Jesus' name, I pray, Amen. <><}*

※※※ ※※※

Jill, Connecticut

The joy of Bible Immersion is this—not missing out on hearing every word that the greatest Lover of our souls has to say to us!

<u>Scripture, Thoughts, Prayer</u>
1 John 4:10 ~ This is love: not that we loved God, but that he loved us and sent his Son as an atoning sacrifice for our sins.

- We are His beloved!
- *{Dear Lord, thank you for Your great love for me. Thank you that You ARE love itself. Thank you that I am loved by You beyond my ability to comprehend it. Open my eyes that I may see marvelous things out of Your law. Create in me a clean heart. Renew a right spirit within me. Open my heart to receive whatever it is you want to say to me. Speak Lord. Your servant is listening. Help me remember that my ways are never better than Yours; they are never more rewarding than Yours. Help me trust You and praise You always. In Jesus name, Amen.}*

Wanda, Maryland

Scripture, Thoughts, Prayer
Matthew 13:22 (NIV) - The seed falling among the thorns refers to someone who hears the word, but the worries of this life and the deceitfulness of wealth choke the word, making it unfruitful.

- Thorns cover the root of the plant and choke out the sunlight so that the plant's full growth never manifests.
- Anxieties over things in my life are thorns. God's word planted in my heart cannot thrive or become fruitful and full grown until I remove the thorns.
- *{Father, thank you for speaking loudly and showing me what has to go in my life, in order for me to grow and to produce your fruit. You are Lord. I want what you want. I am weak, but you are mighty. Help me to see the intangible among the tangible. Thank you for revelation, in Jesus' name. Amen.}*

Lydia, Virginia

If you have prayed to receive Christ and wonder why you have not experienced the change you have wanted, I highly recommend Bible Immersion.

All Christians need to organize their lives—to put Christ in the center. This is called Spiritual Formation. Bible Immersion effectively incorporates three critical disciplines of Spiritual Formation. These are: 1) abiding in Christ (***John 15:5***), 2) continuing in His word (***John 8:31-32***), and 3) praying in faith (***John 15:7***).

Scripture, Thoughts, Prayer
John 15:5 ~ "I am the vine; you are the branches. If you remain in me and I in you, you will bear much fruit; apart from me you can do nothing."

- Bible Immersion facilitates us staying connected to the vine (Jesus).
- Bible Immersion will teach us how to pray according to God's word
- Bible Immersion will enable us to know HIS Word so we can obey HIS Word.

Robin, Ohio

Bible Immersion has provided a way to engage with the word of God in a different way, and to capture items of prayer and thanksgiving.

Scripture, Thoughts, Prayer

Psalm 106:1-2 NLT ~ Praise the Lord! Give thanks to the Lord, for He is good! His faithful love endures forever. Who can list the glorious miracles of the Lord? Who can ever praise Him enough?

- Every good and perfect gift is from God and He alone is worthy of all the praise and honor.
- There is power in praise. Giving thanks is a sacrifice that truly honors Him.
- *{Father, please forgive me for the times I have taken your faithful love and glorious miracles for granted. Father, thank you for who you are, for your word, and for the wonderful gift of abstinence! Lord, it is a gift that I don't ever want to give back or take lightly. Thank you for showing me how I can praise and love you more fervently today.}*

Mary, New York

Bible for Food has been a blessing for me. My life, and eating habits have changed all for the better. Since I started the program I have been inspired and supported by godly women. Sharing and praying with likeminded people it's helped me in all areas of my life.

Scripture, Thoughts, Prayer

John 10:4 ~ When he has brought out all his own, he goes on ahead of them, and his sheep follow him because they know his voice.

- Jesus recognizes His sheep by their voice.
- We know the creator is all holy, good, kind, powerful, and a loving God.
- Greater is He in us then He in the world.

- Our God is amazing and would never lead us to anything ungodly.
- *{Dear Father, thank you for helping and guiding me through life. Thank you for keeping me from going astray. You are merciful and lead me back to you even when I make mistakes. I am a lost sheep without You in my life. It's in Jesus' name that I pray. Amen.}*

Myesha, Maryland

Bible Immersion is a life sustaining force that I need each day. Through doing it I am learning to choose Christ's gift of life over food!

Scripture, Thoughts, Prayer
Deuteronomy 30:19-20 ~ This day I call the heavens and the earth as witnesses against you that I have set before you life and death, blessings and curses. Now choose life, so that you and your children may live and that you may love the Lord your God, listen to his voice, and hold fast to him. For the Lord is your life, and he will give you many years in the land he swore to give to your fathers, Abraham, Isaac and Jacob.

- I choose to receive life, command life, and cherish life in Jesus' name.
- Christ chose us and won the victory over death.
- We have the power to choose Life (Christ) over death. We are warned about which choices brings about which outcomes. The moment by moment question becomes: "Which will you choose?"
- *{Dear Father, You are a promise keeper who shows unfailing love. Help me keep the promise to choose life so that both me and my descendants may live. Show us how to love You Lord. Be*

our God on an intimate ("into-me-you-see") level. Show us how to obey and respond promptly to Your voice. We lay prostrate in awe at your feet—clinging to You, serving You, the length of all our days! Amen.}

※ ※ ※ ※ ※ ※

Barbara, New Jersey

Bible Immersion has helped me understand at a deeper level that the word of God is alive and well in my life. It is not just the information of knowing a Bible verse or being able to find it quickly. Nor is it only about the revelation of knowing what the verse means specifically to me at this time. It is about the transformation that results when I take the word and apply it to my life and live in a different way because of God's word. Praise God!

Scripture, Thoughts, and Prayer
Zephaniah 3:17 ~ The Lord your God is with you, He is mighty to save, He will take great delight in you, He will comfort you with His love, He will rejoice over you with singing.

- God is with me, no matter how I feel.
- God delights in me, no matter how I fail.
- Comfort is available, I need to believe it and receive it.
- *{Lord, help me remember Your presence, Your power and Your provision for me. Everything that happens in my life falls under one of your precious promises. Give me the faith to believe that You are who You say you are and that You will do what You say You will do. Help me believe that I am who You say I am and that I can do all things through Christ who strengthens me because Your Word is alive and active in my life. Lord, I believe, help my unbelief!}*

Diann, New Jersey

Scripture, Thoughts, and Prayer
Matthew 5:8 ~ Blessed are the pure in heart, for they shall see God.

- Something that is pure is unadulterated, not diluted, not dirty. It's just one thing, not a mixture.
- For my heart to be pure it needs to be uncluttered, not bogged down with fear or resentment or negativity, and not filled with all sorts of sinful desires and ambitions.
- If my greatest desire today is for connection with God, then my heart will be pure and I can count on the promise of the last part of the verse, that I will see God.
- I will see Him in my heart, as He enables me to be more keenly aware of His presence, and as He helps me understand and respond in a godly way to the people and circumstances of my life.
- *{Abba, Father, I want to be blessed by You, and I want to see You. I want to have a pure heart of love for You, but I need Your enablement to make that a reality. Please, help me focus on You today. Help me to have You be the one great desire and love of my heart. Help me to turn away from anything that might distract me from pure and unadulterated devotion to You. In Jesus name I pray. Amen!}*

Rebecca, California

(NOTE: Rebecca attended one of the Bible Immersion weekend retreats. A short time later she brought Bible Immersion into a facility where she volunteers. What follows are two examples from those who had just learned about Bible Immersion, followed by her own Scripture, Thoughts, and Prayers.)

Scripture, Thoughts, Prayer (Anonymous)
1 John 4:16 ~ And so we know and rely on the love God has for us. God is love. Whoever lives in love lives in God, and God in them.

- God is Love! This is important to realize—God is Love.
- If we say we love and do not have God (who is Love) then we are being untruthful.
- Love's "standard's" are set by God, since God is Love-This implies there may be ways that God shows love that we are unfamiliar with. To truly know the standards of love, we must truly know God.
- *{God, allow me to understand the love you have for us all, especially your saints. Without that understanding, I will be unable to truly love those I see, ultimately causing me to lack true love for you. Thank you, God, for your love. Thank you in advance for a proper understanding of your love.}*

Scripture, Thoughts, Prayer (Kristina)
1 John 4:20 ~ If anyone boasts, " I love God," and goes right on hating his brother or sister, thinking nothing of it, he is a liar. If he won't love the person he can see, how can he love the God he can't see?

- I underlined verse 20 because I can relate.
- Although, given some thought, I realized that everyone can.
- We all have someone we despise.
- God's son, Jesus, was the only one who was perfect. He was the calm in many storms. (Once, quite literally!)
- So, we are not perfect, but God is. Let's try to follow this.
- *{I pray that I can say I love God without being a liar. I want to be able to love God and forgive my sister and my enemies for the past. I pray that my mother can do this as well. Finally, I pray that I can be the calm in the storm for many or very few.*

It doesn't matter how many. I want to be someone's calm in a storm.}

<u>Scripture, Thoughts, Prayer</u> (Rebecca)
1 John 4: 11-12 ~ Dear friends, since God so loved us, we also ought to love one another. No one has ever seen God; but if we love one another, God lives in us and his love is made complete in us.

- Amazing that such a simple thing as loving one another (and yet so hard to do), causes God to dwell deeply in us, and that His Love completes us—perfects us!
- That is truly mind boggling!
- *{Dear God, I pray that you would continue to perfect me with your love. He who began a good work in me will be faithful to complete it. I repent of reacting and lashing out of self-interest—not out of Love—seeking my own gain and seeking my own rights. I surrender those to you now! Amen. Thank you for forgiving me.}*

These things happened to them as an example, but they were written down for our instruction, on whom the end of the ages has come. ~ 1 Corinthians 10:11

1. TODAY'S DATE _January 19, 2018_

- [x] Write down 1-3 issues that are presently dominating your thoughts and hindering your concentration.

   - reaching today's goals that I have set for productivity
   - that our taxes can be done quickly this year and not at the end in April
   - that I can organize the storage area in the basement

- [x] Ask the Lord to move you away from these concerns, and to center your thoughts on Him. Ask to be filled with the Holy Spirit so that you hear and understand what God is saying in His word.

- [x] On the line below, write your assignment for today (Or choose 3 new Bible chapters to read.)

   Genesis 46-47; Matthew 12:22-50

- [x] Find an audio version of your reading assignment.
- [x] While listening and reading, underline anything that catches your attention.
- [x] Choose a verse, write down the address, and a few primary words from which will be your area of concentration.
- [x] Journal on: (a) What comes to mind when reading over your Scripture selection, and/or (b) What might God be saying to you regarding your life and your issues in the light of these Scriptures?
- [x] Write a prayer, and then pray it aloud to the Lord.
- [ ] If time allows, share your insights in a "Scripture, Thoughts, Prayer" format with others.

28

Daily Page Example

Matthew 12:32 — and whoever speaks a word against the Son of Man will be forgiven, but whoever speaks against the Holy Spirit will not be forgiven, either in this age or in the age to come.

[I have heard people swear by the name of Jesus and realize that many are people-pleasing and fearful.]

[Some are attempting to look big before others. They are among the ones that Jesus says: "Forgive them for they know not what they are doing!"]

[Then there are those who do know what they are doing. They have experienced the prompting by the Holy Spirit, yet they choose to pretend that they haven't.]

[There are those who have hardened their hearts and have sealed their doom!]

Hebrews 3:15 — ... today, if you hear His voice, do not harden your hearts ...

Dear Father, sin deceives. Strengthen

Daily Page Example

me to live truth today and to speak it. Please reach the hearts of those close by. I pray not to give in to discouragement, but to pray hard for their salvation!

Genesis 46:1-4 ~ "... So Israel took his journey with all that he had..."

There is an excitement about being in a new environment, but there is also the loss of order that can feel unsettling.

The good news is that Jacob and his family had God on their side! He was going to be their guide and protector.

~ "... do not be afraid to go down to Egypt, for there I will make you into a great nation. I myself will go down with you to Egypt..."

Dear Father, You are always with me, too! I cannot be where You are not. I pray to make the time to be still. Fill me with Your presence. In this very hour, let me know that You are near.

Daily Page Example

✿ NOTES, PLANS, AND PRAYERS FOR OTHERS ✿

(Prayers for Others)

- Anita: concern for her daughter and the choices she has been making

- Crystal: that the Lord will give her the willingness and strength again to be disciplined with her food.

- Sam: (Kayla's son) that he will do excellently at his interview and get the job.

(Notes from sweet radio sermon on forgiveness)

- We do not forgive in our own power.
- It can only be sustained in the power of Christ.
- It requires much prayer.

{Dear Father, one day Jesus will come back to take me to be where He is *(John 14: 3)*. As I wait His return, I pray to live a life that pleases You. Please keep me immersed in Your word each day. Please keep me trained and equipped---teaching others to do the same. In the name of Jesus I pray. Amen.}

31

Daily Page Example

January

1	☐ Genesis 1-2	☐ Matthew 1
2	☐ Genesis 3-4	☐ Matthew 2
3	☐ Genesis 5-8	☐ Matthew 3
4	☐ Genesis 9-11	☐ Matthew 4
5	☐ Genesis 12-15	☐ Matthew 5:1-26
6	☐ Genesis 16-18	☐ Matthew 5:27-48
7	☐ Genesis 19-20	☐ Matthew 6:1-18
8	☐ Genesis 21-23	☐ Matthew 6:19-34
9	☐ Genesis 24-25	☐ Matthew 7:1-14
10	☐ Genesis 26-27	☐ Matthew 7:15-29
11	☐ Genesis 28-29	☐ Matthew 8:1-17
12	☐ Genesis 30-31	☐ Matthew 8:18-34
13	☐ Genesis 32-33	☐ Matthew 9:1-17
14	☐ Genesis 34-36	☐ Matthew 9:18-38
15	☐ Genesis 37-38	☐ Matthew 10:1-15
16	☐ Genesis 39-41	☐ Matthew 10:16-42
17	☐ Genesis 42-43	☐ Matthew 11
18	☐ Genesis 44-45	☐ Matthew 12:1-21
19	☐ Genesis 46-47	☐ Matthew 12:22-50
20	☐ Genesis 48-50	☐ Matthew 13:1-23
21	☐ Exodus 1-2	☐ Matthew 13:24-43
22	☐ Exodus 3-4	☐ Matthew 13:44-58
23	☐ Exodus 5-7	☐ Matthew 14
24	☐ Exodus 8-10	☐ Matthew 15:1-20
25	☐ Exodus 11-12	☐ Matthew 15:21-39
26	☐ Exodus 13-14	☐ Matthew 16
27	☐ Exodus 15-16	☐ Matthew 17
28	☐ Exodus 17-19	☐ Matthew 18
29	☐ Exodus 20-22	☐ Matthew 19:1-15
30	☐ Exodus 23-25	☐ Matthew 19:16-30
31	☐ Exodus 26-27	☐ Matthew 20:1-19

February

1	☐ Exodus 28-30	☐ Matthew 20:20-34
2	☐ Exodus 31-32	☐ Matthew 21:1-22
3	☐ Exodus 33-34	☐ Matthew 21:23-46
4	☐ Exodus 35-36	☐ Matthew 22:1-22
5	☐ Exodus 37-38	☐ Matthew 22:23-46
6	☐ Exodus 39-40	☐ Matthew 23
7	☐ Leviticus 1-4	☐ Matthew 24
8	☐ Leviticus 5-7	☐ Matthew 25:1-30
9	☐ Leviticus 8-9	☐ Matthew 25:31-46
10	☐ Leviticus 10-11	☐ Matthew 26:1-35
11	☐ Leviticus 12-13	☐ Matthew 26:36-75
12	☐ Leviticus 14-15	☐ Matthew 27:1-31
13	☐ Leviticus 16-17	☐ Matthew 27:32-66
14	☐ Leviticus 18-19	☐ Matthew 28
15	☐ Leviticus 20-22	☐ Mark 1:1-28
16	☐ Leviticus 23-24	☐ Mark 1:29-45
17	☐ Leviticus 25	☐ Mark 2
18	☐ Leviticus 26-27	☐ Mark 3
19	☐ Numbers 1-2	☐ Mark 4:1-20
20	☐ Numbers 3-4	☐ Mark 4:21-41
21	☐ Numbers 5-6	☐ Mark 5:1-20
22	☐ Numbers 7	☐ Mark 5:21-43
23	☐ Numbers 8-9	☐ Mark 6:1-29
24	☐ Numbers 10-11	☐ Mark 6:30-56
25	☐ Numbers 12-14	☐ Mark 7:1-23
26	☐ Numbers 15-16	☐ Mark 7:24-37
27	☐ Numbers 17-18	☐ Mark 8
28	☐ Numbers 19-20	☐ Mark 9:1-29
29	☐ Read 3 chapters of your choice	

March

1	☐ Numbers 21-22	☐ Mark 9:30-50
2	☐ Numbers 23-25	☐ Mark 10:1-31
3	☐ Numbers 26-27	☐ Mark 10:32-52
4	☐ Numbers 28-30	☐ Mark 11:1-19
5	☐ Numbers 31	☐ Mark 11:20-33
6	☐ Numbers 32-34	☐ Mark 12:1-27
7	☐ Numbers 35-36	☐ Mark 12:28-44
8	☐ Deuteronomy 1-2	☐ Mark 13:1-23
9	☐ Deuteronomy 3-4	☐ Mark 13:24-37
10	☐ Deuteronomy 5-6	☐ Mark 14:1-31
11	☐ Deuteronomy 7-9	☐ Mark 14:32-72
12	☐ Deuteronomy 10-11	☐ Mark 15:1-32
13	☐ Deuteronomy 12-14	☐ Mark 15:33-47
14	☐ Deuteronomy 15-16	☐ Mark 16
15	☐ Deuteronomy 17-19	☐ Luke 1:1-25
16	☐ Deuteronomy 20-22	☐ Luke 1:26-56
17	☐ Deuteronomy 23-25	☐ Luke 1:57-80
18	☐ Deuteronomy 26-27	☐ Luke 2:1-21
19	☐ Deuteronomy 28	☐ Luke 2:22-52
20	☐ Deuteronomy 29-31	☐ Luke 3:1-22
21	☐ Deuteronomy 32	☐ Luke 3:23-38
22	☐ Deuteronomy 33-34	☐ Luke 4:1-30
23	☐ Joshua 1-3	☐ Luke 4:31-44
24	☐ Joshua 4-6	☐ Luke 5:1-16
25	☐ Joshua 7-8	☐ Luke 5:17-39
26	☐ Joshua 9-10	☐ Luke 6:1-19
27	☐ Joshua 11-13	☐ Luke 6:20-36
28	☐ Joshua 14-15	☐ Luke 6:37-49
29	☐ Joshua 16-18	☐ Luke 7:1-17
30	☐ Joshua 19-21	☐ Luke 7:18-35
31	☐ Joshua 22	☐ Luke 7:36-50

April

1	☐ Joshua 23-24	☐ Luke 8:1-25
2	☐ Judges 1-2	☐ Luke 8:26-56
3	☐ Judges 3-4	☐ Luke 9:1-17
4	☐ Judges 5-6	☐ Luke 9:18-45
5	☐ Judges 7-8	☐ Luke 9:46-62
6	☐ Judges 9-10	☐ Luke 10:1-24
7	☐ Judges 11-12	☐ Luke 10:25-42
8	☐ Judges 13-15	☐ Luke 11:1-32
9	☐ Judges 16-17	☐ Luke 11:33-54
10	☐ Judges 18-19	☐ Luke 12:1-21

11	☐ Judges 20-21 ☐ Luke 12:22-48	
12	☐ Ruth 1-4 ☐ Luke 12:49-59	
13	☐ 1 Samuel 1-2 ☐ Luke 13:1-17	
14	☐ 1 Samuel 3-4 ☐ Luke 13:18-35	
15	☐ 1 Samuel 5-8 ☐ Luke 14	
16	☐ 1 Samuel 9-10 ☐ Luke 15	
17	☐ 1 Samuel 11-13 ☐ Luke 16	
18	☐ 1 Samuel 14 ☐ Luke 17:1-19	
19	☐ 1 Samuel 15-16 ☐ Luke 17:20-37	
20	☐ 1 Samuel 17-18 ☐ Luke 18	
21	☐ 1 Samuel 19-20 ☐ Luke 19:1-27	
22	☐ 1 Samuel 21-23 ☐ Luke 19:28-48	
23	☐ 1 Samuel 24-25 ☐ Luke 20:1-18	
24	☐ 1 Samuel 26-28 ☐ Luke 20:19-47	
25	☐ 1 Samuel 29-31 ☐ Luke 21	
26	☐ 2 Samuel 1-2 ☐ Luke 22:1-23	
27	☐ 2 Samuel 3-4 ☐ Luke 22:24-46	
28	☐ 2 Samuel 5-7 ☐ Luke 22:47-71	
29	☐ 2 Samuel 8-10 ☐ Luke 23:1-25	
30	☐ 2 Samuel 11-12 ☐ Luke 23:26-56	

May

1	☐ 2 Samuel 13-14 ☐ Luke 24:1-12
2	☐ 2 Samuel 15-16 ☐ Luke 24:13-53
3	☐ 2 Samuel 17-18 ☐ John 1:1-28
4	☐ 2 Samuel 19 ☐ John 1:29-51
5	☐ 2 Samuel 20-21 ☐ John 2
6	☐ 2 Samuel 22 ☐ John 3:1-21
7	☐ 2 Samuel 23-24 ☐ John 3:22-36
8	☐ 1 Kings 1-2 ☐ John 4:1-45
9	☐ 1 Kings 3-4 ☐ John 4:56-54
10	☐ 1 Kings 5-6 ☐ John 5:1-29
11	☐ 1Kings 7 ☐ John 5:30-47
12	☐ 1 Kings 8 ☐ John 6:1-21
13	☐ 1 Kings 9-11 ☐ John 6:22-71
14	☐ 1 Kings 12 ☐ John 7:1-24
15	☐ 1 Kings 13-14 ☐ John 7:25-53
16	☐ 1 Kings 15-16 ☐ John 8:1-30
17	☐ 1 Kings 17-18 ☐ John 8:31-59
18	☐ 1 Kings 19-20 ☐ John 9
19	☐ 1 Kings 21-22 ☐ John 10:1-21
20	☐ 2 Kings 1-2 ☐ John 10:22-42
21	☐ 2 Kings 3 ☐ John 11:1-37
22	☐ 2 Kings 4-5 ☐ John 11:38-57
23	☐ 2 Kings 6-7 ☐ John 12:1-26
24	☐ 2 Kings 8-9 ☐ John 12:27-50
25	☐ 2 Kings 10-11 ☐ John 13:1-20
26	☐ 2 Kings 12-13 ☐ John 13:21-38
27	☐ 2 Kings 14-15 ☐ John 14
28	☐ 2 Kings 16-17 ☐ John 15
29	☐ 2 Kings 18-19 ☐ John 16
30	☐ 2 Kings 20-22 ☐ John 17
31	☐ 2 Kings 23 ☐ John 18:1-18

June

1	☐ 2 Kings 24-25 ☐ John 18:19-40
2	☐ 1 Chronicles 1-3 ☐ John 19:1-16
3	☐ 1 Chronicles 4-5 ☐ John 19:17-42
4	☐ 1 Chronicles 6-7 ☐ John 20:1-18
5	☐ 1 Chronicles 8-11 ☐ John 20:19-30
6	☐ 1 Chronicles 12-13 ☐ John 21:1-14
7	☐ 1 Chronicles 14-16 ☐ John 21:15-25
8	☐ 1 Chronicles 17-19 ☐ Acts 1
9	☐ 1 Chronicles 20-22 ☐ Acts 2:1-13
10	☐ 1 Chronicles 23-25 ☐ Acts 2:14-47
11	☐ 1 Chronicles 26-27 ☐ Acts 3
12	☐ 1 Chronicles 28-29 ☐ Acts 4:1-22
13	☐ 2 Chronicles 1-3 ☐ Acts 4:23-37
14	☐ 2 Chronicles 4-6 ☐ Acts 5:1-16
15	☐ 2 Chronicles 7-8 ☐ Acts 5:17-42
16	☐ 2 Chronicles 9-11 ☐ Acts 6
17	☐ 2 Chronicles 12-16 ☐ Acts 7:1-53
18	☐ 2 Chronicles 17-18 ☐ Acts 7:54-60
19	☐ 2 Chronicles 19-20 ☐ Acts 8:1-25
20	☐ 2 Chronicles 21-23 ☐ Acts 8:26-40
21	☐ 2 Chronicles 24-26 ☐ Acts 9:1-22
22	☐ 2 Chronicles 27-29 ☐ Acts 9:23-43
23	☐ 2 Chronicles 30-31 ☐ Acts 10:1-33
24	☐ 2 Chronicles 32 ☐ Acts 10:34-48
25	☐ 2 Chronicles 33-34 ☐ Acts 11
26	☐ 2 Chronicles 35-36 ☐ Acts 12
27	☐ Ezra 1-3 ☐ Acts 13:1-12
28	☐ Ezra 4-6 ☐ Acts 13:13-52
29	☐ Ezra 7-8 ☐ Acts 14
30	☐ Ezra 9-10 ☐ Acts 15:1-21

July

1	☐ Nehemiah 1-3 ☐ Act 15:22-41
2	☐ Nehemiah 4-6 ☐ Act 16:1-15
3	☐ Nehemiah 7-8 ☐ Act 16:16-40
4	☐ Nehemiah 9-10 ☐ Act 17:1-21
5	☐ Nehemiah 11-12 ☐ Act 17:22-34
6	☐ Nehemiah 13 ☐ Act 18
7	☐ Esther 1-4 ☐ Act 19:1-20
8	☐ Esther 5-8 ☐ Act 19:21-42
9	☐ Esther 9-10 ☐ Act 20:1-16
10	☐ Job 1-4 ☐ Act 20:17-38
11	☐ Job 5-8 ☐ Act 21:1-26
12	☐ Job 9-12 ☐ Acts 21:27-40
13	☐ Job 13-15 ☐ Act 22
14	☐ Job 16-18 ☐ Act 23:1-11
15	☐ Job 19-21 ☐ Acts 23:12-35
16	☐ Job 22-24 ☐ Acts 24
17	☐ Job 25-28 ☐ Acts 25
18	☐ Job 29-31 ☐ Acts 26:1-11
19	☐ Job 32-33 ☐ Acts 26:12-32
20	☐ Job 34-36 ☐ Acts 27:1-12
21	☐ Job 37-38 ☐ Acts 27:13-44

22	☐ Job 39-42 ☐ Acts 28:1-16	
23	☐ Psalm 1-6 ☐ Acts 28:17-31	
24	☐ Psalm 7-9 ☐ Romans 1:1-17	
25	☐ Psalm 10-16 ☐ Romans 1:18-32	
26	☐ Psalm 17-18 ☐ Romans 2	
27	☐ Psalm 19-21 ☐ Romans 3	
28	☐ Psalm 22-25 ☐ Romans 4	
29	☐ Psalm 26-30 ☐ Romans 5	
30	☐ Psalm 31-33 ☐ Romans 6	
31	☐ Psalm 34-36 ☐ Romans 7	

August

1	☐ Psalm 37-39 ☐ Romans 8:1-17
2	☐ Psalm 40-44 ☐ Romans 8:18-39
3	☐ Psalm 45-48 ☐ Romans 9
4	☐ Psalm 49-52 ☐ Romans 10
5	☐ Psalm 53-57 ☐ Romans 11:1-10
6	☐ Psalm 58-62 ☐ Romans 11:11-36
7	☐ Psalm 63-67 ☐ Romans 12
8	☐ Psalm 68-69 ☐ Romans 13
9	☐ Psalm 70-72 ☐ Romans 14
10	☐ Psalm 73-77 ☐ Romans 15:1-21
11	☐ Psalm 78 ☐ Romans 15:22-33
12	☐ Psalm 79-82 ☐ Romans 16
13	☐ Psalm 83-87 ☐ 1 Corinthians 1
14	☐ Psalm 88-89 ☐ 1 Corinthians 2
15	☐ Psalm 90-95 ☐ 1 Corinthians 3
16	☐ Psalm 96-101 ☐ 1 Corinthians 4
17	☐ Psalm 102-104 ☐ 1 Corinthians 5
18	☐ Psalm 105 ☐ 1 Corinthians 6
19	☐ Psalm 106-107 ☐ 1 Corinthians 7
20	☐ Psalm 108-112 ☐ 1 Corinthians 8
21	☐ Psalm 113-118 ☐ 1 Corinthians 9
22	☐ Psalm 119 ☐ 1 Corinthians 10
23	☐ Psalm 120-125 ☐ 1 Corinthians 11
24	☐ Psalm 126-134 ☐ 1 Corinthians 12
25	☐ Psalm 135-138 ☐ 1 Corinthians 13
26	☐ Psalm 139-142 ☐ 1 Corinthians 14:1-25
27	☐ Psalm 143-146 ☐ 1 Corinthians 14:26-40
28	☐ Psalm 147-150 ☐ 1 Corinthians 15:1-34
29	☐ Proverbs 1-3 ☐ 1 Corinthians 15:35-58
30	☐ Proverbs 4-6 ☐ 1 Corinthians 16
31	☐ Proverbs 7-9 ☐ 2 Corinthians 1

September

1	☐ Proverbs 10-12 ☐ 2 Corinthians 2
2	☐ Proverbs 13-15 ☐ 2 Corinthians 3
3	☐ Proverbs 16-17 ☐ 2 Corinthians 4
4	☐ Proverbs 18-20 ☐ 2 Corinthians 5
5	☐ Proverbs 21-23 ☐ 2 Corinthians 6
6	☐ Proverbs 24-25 ☐ 2 Corinthians 7
7	☐ Proverbs 26-28 ☐ 2 Corinthians 8
8	☐ Proverbs 29-31 ☐ 2 Corinthians 9
9	☐ Ecclesiastes 1-2 ☐ 2 Corinthians 10
10	☐ Ecclesiastes 3-6 ☐ 2 Corinthians 11
11	☐ Ecclesiastes 7-9 ☐ 2 Corinthians 12
12	☐ Ecclesiastes 10-12 ☐ 2 Corinthians 13
13	☐ Song of Songs 1-4 ☐ Galatians 1
14	☐ Song of Songs 5-8 ☐ Galatians 2
15	☐ Isaiah 1-2 ☐ Galatians 3:1-14
16	☐ Isaiah 3-4 ☐ Galatians 3: 15-29
17	☐ Isaiah 5-6 ☐ Galatians 4
18	☐ Isaiah 7-9 ☐ Galatians 5
19	☐ Isaiah 10-11 ☐ Galatians 6
20	☐ Isaiah 12-14 ☐ Ephesians 1
21	☐ Isaiah 15-17 ☐ Ephesians 2
22	☐ Isaiah 18-20 ☐ Ephesians 3
23	☐ Isaiah 21-23 ☐ Ephesians 4
24	☐ Isaiah 24-26 ☐ Ephesians 5
25	☐ Isaiah 27-28 ☐ Ephesians 6
26	☐ Isaiah 29-30 ☐ Philippians 1
27	☐ Isaiah 31-32 ☐ Philippians 2
28	☐ Isaiah 33-35 ☐ Philippians 3
29	☐ Isaiah 36-37 ☐ Philippians 4
30	☐ Isaiah 38-40 ☐ Colossians 1

October

1	☐ Isaiah 41 ☐ Colossians 2
2	☐ Isaiah 42-43 ☐ Colossians 3
3	☐ Isaiah 44-45 ☐ Colossians 4
4	☐ Isaiah 46-48 ☐ 1 Thessalonians 1
5	☐ Isaiah 49-50 ☐ 1 Thessalonians 2
6	☐ Isaiah 51-52 ☐ 1 Thessalonians 3
7	☐ Isaiah 53-55 ☐ 1 Thessalonians 4
8	☐ Isaiah 56-57 ☐ 1 Thessalonians 5
9	☐ Isaiah 58-60 ☐ 2 Thessalonians 1
10	☐ Isaiah 61-62 ☐ 2 Thessalonians 2
11	☐ Isaiah 63-64 ☐ 2 Thessalonians 3
12	☐ Isaiah 65-66 ☐ 1 Timothy 1
13	☐ Jeremiah 1-2 ☐ 1 Timothy 2
14	☐ Jeremiah 3-4 ☐ 1 Timothy 3
15	☐ Jeremiah 5 ☐ 1 Timothy 4
16	☐ Jeremiah 6-7 ☐ 1 Timothy 5
17	☐ Jeremiah 8-9 ☐ 1 Timothy 6
18	☐ Jeremiah 10-11 ☐ 2 Timothy 1
19	☐ Jeremiah 12-13 ☐ 2 Timothy 2
20	☐ Jeremiah 14-15 ☐ 2 Timothy 3
21	☐ Jeremiah 16-18 ☐ 2 Timothy 4
22	☐ Jeremiah 19-21 ☐ Titus 1
23	☐Jeremiah 22 ☐ Titus 2
24	☐ Jeremiah 23-24 ☐ Titus 3
25	☐ Jeremiah 25-26 ☐ Philemon 1
26	☐ Jeremiah 27-29 ☐ Hebrews 1
27	☐ Jeremiah 30-31 ☐ Hebrews 2
28	☐ Jeremiah 32 ☐ Hebrews 3
29	☐ Jeremiah 33-35 ☐ Hebrews 4
30	☐ Jeremiah 36-37 ☐ Hebrews 5
31	☐ Jeremiah 38-40 ☐ Hebrews 6

November

1	☐ Jeremiah 41-43 ☐ Hebrews 7:1-10
2	☐ Jeremiah 44-46 ☐ Hebrews 7:11-28
3	☐ Jeremiah 47-48 ☐ Hebrews 8
4	☐ Jeremiah 49 ☐ Hebrews 9:1-10
5	☐ Jeremiah 50 ☐ Hebrews 9:11-28
6	☐ Jeremiah 51 ☐ Hebrews 10:1-18
7	☐ Jeremiah 52 ☐ Hebrews 10:19-39
8	☐ Lamentations 1 ☐ Hebrews 11
9	☐ Lamentations 2 ☐ Hebrews 12:1-17
10	☐ Lamentations 3 ☐ Hebrews 12:18-29
11	☐ Lamentations 4-5 ☐ Hebrews 13
12	☐ Ezekiel 1-3 ☐ James 1
13	☐ Ezekiel 4-7 ☐ James 2
14	☐ Ezekiel 8-11 ☐ James 3
15	☐ Ezekiel 12-14 ☐ James 4
16	☐ Ezekiel 15-16 ☐ James 5
17	☐ Ezekiel 17-18 ☐ 1 Peter 1
18	☐ Ezekiel 19-20 ☐ 1 Peter 2:1-12
19	☐ Ezekiel 21-22 ☐ 1 Peter 2:13-25
20	☐ Ezekiel 23-24 ☐ 1 Peter 3
21	☐ Ezekiel 25-27 ☐ 1 Peter 4
22	☐ Ezekiel 28-29 ☐ 1 Peter 5
23	☐ Ezekiel 30-31 ☐ 2 Peter 1
24	☐ Ezekiel 32-33 ☐ 2 Peter 2
25	☐ Ezekiel 34-35 ☐ 2 Peter 3
26	☐ Ezekiel 36-37 ☐ 1 John 1
27	☐ Ezekiel 38-39 ☐ 1 John 2:1-14
28	☐ Ezekiel 40-41 ☐ 1 John 2:15-29
29	☐ Ezekiel 42-44 ☐ 1 John 3:1-10
30	☐ Ezekiel 45-46 ☐ 1 John 3:11-20

December

1	☐ Ezekiel 47-48 ☐ 1 John 4
2	☐ Daniel 1-2 ☐ 1 John 5
3	☐ Daniel 3-4 ☐ 2 John 1
4	☐ Daniel 5 ☐ 3 John 1
5	☐ Daniel 6-7 ☐ Jude 1
6	☐ Daniel 8-9 ☐ Revelation 1
7	☐ Daniel 10-12 ☐ Revelation 2:1-11
8	☐ Hosea 1-2 ☐ Revelation 2:12-29
9	☐ Hosea 3-6 ☐ Revelation 3
10	☐ Hosea 7-10 ☐ Revelation 4
11	☐ Hosea 11-14 ☐ Revelation 5
12	☐ Joel 1-2 ☐ Revelation 6
13	☐ Joel 3 ☐ Revelation 7:1-8
14	☐ Amos 1-2 ☐ Revelation 7:9-17
15	☐ Amos 3-5 ☐ Revelation 8
16	☐ Amos 6-7 ☐ Revelation 9
17	☐ Amos 8-9 ☐ Revelation 10
18	☐ Obadiah 1 ☐ Revelation 11
19	☐ Jonah 1-4 ☐ Revelation 12
20	☐ Micah 1-3 ☐ Revelation 13
21	☐ Micah 4-5 ☐ Revelation 14
22	☐ Micah 6-7 ☐ Revelation 15
23	☐ Nahum 1-3 ☐ Revelation 16
24	☐ Habakkuk 1-3 ☐ Revelation 17
25	☐ Zephaniah 1-3 ☐ Revelation 18
26	☐ Haggai 1-2 ☐ Revelation 19:1-10
27	☐ Zachariah 1-4 ☐ Revelation 19:11-21
28	☐ Zachariah 5-8 ☐ Revelation 20
29	☐ Zachariah 9-11 ☐ Revelation 21:1-8
30	☐ Zachariah 12-14 ☐ Revelation 21:9-27
31	☐ Malachi 1-4 ☐ Revelation 22

CPSIA information can be obtained
at www.ICGtesting.com
Printed in the USA
BVHW072001131121
621495BV00001B/37